Seasons of the Soul

To Tracy & Curtis,

may God's grace fill

the seasons of your life

Carol Gura

Seasons of the Soul

CAROL GURA

*Discover the sacredness of life
and life's experiences*

ThomasMore®
Allen, Texas

Send all inquiries to:

THOMAS MORE PUBLISHING
200 East Bethany Drive
Allen, Texas 75002-3804

Telephone: 877-275-4725 / 972-390-6300

Fax: 800-688-8356 / 972-390-6560

E-mail: **cservice@rcl-enterprises.com**

Website: **www.thomasmore.com**

Printed in the United States of America

Library of Congress Catalog Number 2001086062

ISBN 0-88347-469-7

1 2 3 4 5   05 04 03 02 01

DEDICATION

To my grandchildren, Elizabeth
and Ryan, whose innocence and
simplicity open my eyes to see and
center me on this path of the soul

Acknowledgments

Once again, I thank my husband Bob, whose gentle hold on my soul spins me out into the unknown, yet grounds me in truth and steadfast love. My gratitude extends to those who set me on this path into the spiritual over the years, those many teachers and mentors too numerous to name, beginning with my parents, Ann and Anton, and to those men and women who listen to my musings about the soul's journey in workshops and retreats, encouraging me to continue in their affirmation and appreciation. My heart fills with deep thanks for my family: Don, Trisha, Elizabeth, Rob, Jill, Laurel, Joel, and Ryan. Their understanding of my work and insights on this spiritual path pepper the pages of this book with humor, depth, and breadth. The publishers and editors at Thomas More Publishing and Resources for Christian Living have encouraged and directed me with their knowledge of this complex world of publishing yet have continually respected and reverenced my most authentic creative spirit.

Contents

Winter

Introduction

We live interrupted lives. Overstimulated by multiple tasks and snarled in the disconnected threads of too many choices and multilayered experiences, we are exhausted. The mobility of modern culture leaves us adrift with feelings of longing as we seek to lay down roots. Our dreams of meaningful work are catapulted by downsizing, right-sizing, and eventually outsizing. It is no wonder that we experience disease with the way life has gone for us. This discontinuity has caused people of this modern, first-world culture to embark upon an authentic search for meaning, wholeness, and healing. We have finally faced the fact that we cannot recapture the exhilaration of the post-war era, or the dizzying escapes of the hippie movement. The age of affluence, spending, and consuming of the eighties did not satisfy our deepest desires. Nor did a headlong thrust into an egocentric frenzy over improving the self in the nineties fulfill the inner longing that cries out from the depths of the human hearts—ultimately, from the core of the universe.

Stripped down to the core of our being, we are ready to risk the headlong plunge into the spiritual journey of soul seekers. All cries out to be transformed, to be healed, and to be made whole once again. The collective voice of women and men form a living body, an animated soul that longs to recover that which lies within. The earth cries out in union with the human spirit, not for restoration but for transformation, healing and wholeness. Together, humankind and all the created universe desire to have her creative energies liberated from the fragmentation, the interruptions, and the discontinuities that plague modern living. But we already have learned that we will not succeed in this quest if we escape into the consuming patterns of hoarding and having. We cannot rely upon our own ego-feeding or willpower or accomplishments to satisfy the human hunger for meaning. We are on this journey together as a human, living body, as a communion of all creatures, and as a living organism called the cosmos.

This book is written with the intention of looking into the patterns found in nature's seasons in order to discover the sacredness of all of life and life's experiences. Women and men, together, seek to discover spiritual truth and growth by drawing from nature in her seasons of ebbing and flowing, living and dying, birthing and regenerating. In the seasons of nature we find a mirror that reflects the patterns in our spiritual path to the Unknown. Members of one living body, animated by the same Spirit, we can break open the blocked corners of the Spirit within in order to release the transformative power of the soul of the universe.

There is a hidden beauty beneath the surface of each person. This is the beauty of the soul. Spirituality is a journey inward to uncover that beauty. The most ordinary aspects of our lives hold the potential to retrieve that beauty, that soul, in order to give birth to a new vision, which can transform the world.

We are here to set our inner light aflame—to grow our soul. The soul is the soil from which we came and into which we are going. But in the here and now we are co-creating, co-laboring with God, a Higher Being, the Creator or whatever name we prefer, to hone and refine that which is our spark of life. Today it is easier to write a resumé than it is to develop our soul. It is easier to keep going, to keep busy in order to avoid the inner loneliness, than it is to get a real life. Real living is an adventure. It takes risk, struggle, and great courage. We might not know where we are headed, but the point, after all, is the journey!

This is a journey into the realms of the soul. Meister Eckhert said, "Every creature is a book about God!" Does it not then make sense to cultivate, to discover, and to seek the image of God within all of life's creatures? Human, plant and animal, rock and wind, earth and sun all reveal the mystery of the divine if we but learn the language and decipher the patterns. I am convinced that this trek into the soul of life itself is a pilgrimage back to the Source, the ultimate purpose of our existence. Self-improvement, material possessions, and job security will never satisfy. Only the daily walk through suffering and joy, pain and ecstasy, boredom and loneliness with eyes wide open can place us on the course for which we were always intended.

USING THIS BOOK

The four seasons: spring, summer, autumn, and winter provide a lens through which we can perceive some basic spiritual truths on this pilgrimage of the soul. Spring begins the walk with an eye wide open to the sacredness of all of life. By learning to cultivate the art of "seeing" we can grow our souls into understanding the meaning of all that exists. Summer helps us focus upon the connectedness of all of life. When we recover our sense of communion we can begin to recover and reintegrate our fractured lives into the wholeness of a seamless garment. The gleaming, gleaning time of autumn invites the soul to recognize the giftedness that lies within and to live in gracious gratitude. Generous hearts are free to give and receive the bounty of the earth. Wisdom is winter's spiritual truth. To come to the season of recognizing mortality, cultivating imagination, and trusting intuition leads the soul to embrace authentic wisdom. With wisdom one comes to know, to hope, and to trust in the ultimate Source of the Soul.

The short reflections on these themes are intended to be read and reflected upon for a day or several days. There is no need to rush through the stories, essays, and poems that ensue. Take each for its impact upon your experiences of life. If it is helpful, journal your thoughts, poems, and questions that emerge in the section that follows each reflection. In the center of each season is a *meditation* that affords an opportunity to focus on the themes that emerge. Use this centering reflection several times if you find it effective. You might also choose to use it as a catalyst for your own meditation time. The important task of the spiritual journey is to spend time

in quiet reflection. There is suggested *ritual action* at the end
of each season. Rituals take us beyond the ordinary, making
the connections beyond the personal. The action of ritual-
izing taps into the source of power and energy that
transforms the soul. Try the suggested rituals either at the
end of each season or throughout the days of reflection,
repeating them several times.

The journey of the soul is cultivated in an authentic,
seeking heart. It is not a journey of perfection, but rather one
of gleaning out the truth in the imperfections of life. It is not
a journey of warm, fuzzy feelings, but rather a bold and
courageous attempt to risk unmasking the meaning, purpose,
and culmination of life. Perhaps this poem captures the
essence of this soul search.

"I"

I, the only one responsible for this sojourn
the one alone who can make meaning
> make hope
>> make sense of each moment . . . a dot
> on the days, months, and years of this existence.
"I," the one who alone pushed through
> the womb to life
>> and will alone thrust into
>>> the life that awaits.
The "I" of Integration and Insight
> that stirs me into wholeness;
of Imagination and Intuition
> that spins me into mysteries beyond my dreams;
of Incarnation and Introspection
> that guides me in understanding the complexities
>> that surround me;
of Interdependence and Intricacy
> that binds me in this fine-spun web of life.
"I," the really real!
> "I," the soul—a pulsing star in the Soul of the Universe.

Spring

INTRODUCTION

When all our daily experiences and encounters are infused with reverence, everything comes alive. There is meaning, understanding, and hope as we begin to really see. "Seeing is believing" is the wisdom found in the well-worn adage. The first step to renewing the inner spirit is to cultivate the art of seeing, not just observing but to detect, discover and perceive. To see is to understand, to grasp and to come to know the purpose and meaning of life's varied and wonderful treasures. Not just your own individual personal life, but the meaning of all life—the whys and wherefores of life, the reality of being, the vivacity of the soul and the sustenance of the universe. Spring is the season of seeing. Read and ponder "The Salutation to the Dawn" found in the *Hindu Vedas* and discover how crucial it is to be awake and conscious—to really see.

Look to this day
For it is life.
The very life of life.
In its brief course lie all
The realities and verities of existence.
The bliss of growth.
The splendor of action.
The glory of power.
For yesterday is but a dream,
And tomorrow is only a vision.
But today, well lived,
Makes every yesterday a dream of happiness
And every tomorrow a vision of hope.
Look well, therefore, to this day.

SOFTEN ME

Soft spring winds
curve around the cup of my hand
   thrust from an open window.
Driving through country roads,
   caught in that magical moment
   just before expectant green shoots penetrate the earth,
     dredged with manure—
    an aroma of musk, fresh and ripe,
  cuts the air with acrid scent.
The utter soft freshness of it all
   blows in and out my soul, open vessel
welcoming the bliss of spring's newness.
Wash over me, winds of change;
   round out the sharp angles of anger,
piercing daggers of distrust,
     barbs of bitterness that lie dormant within.
Spring, blow through the jagged crevices of my spirit
with your life-giving power to smooth my soul,
stretching me in your caressing winds,
   laden with first fragrance of hyacinth,
   purpled pleasantly in the rooks of roadway rock.

               ❧

The Harbingers of Spring
Walk through nature to learn her secret wisdom.
What messages do the harbingers of spring bring
to your inner spirit?

THE SMALLEST

There was a fly in the kitchen. The mother of four-year-old Elizabeth wadded up the newspaper, raising her hand to strike a deathblow. The child howled, "Mommy, what are you doing? You'll kill it!" Hand in midair, mom shooed the fly to the door, opened it, and let it escape to do its fly "thing." She couldn't bear to deal with all the "Why's?" that would surely follow if she had made her mark.

Several days later the two were knee-deep in mud, planting early peas in the wet soil. The child toiled next to her mommy, donning two large garden gloves so as to keep her hands clean and free of the black earth. One deep plunge into the sweet loam revealed an earthworm, which entranced little Elizabeth. She immediately tore off the gloves, begging to hold the worm. It wriggled around her pudgy fingers, delighting her with tickles. This began the search for more worms to hold as holy bread or sacred sacrament.

The smallest of creatures are tracings of the sacred on our planet. Noticed through the eyes of a child, these small details of nature can stir us to wonder and awe. This is the reverence required by the *Great Mother*. This is the stuff of the soul. This is the art of truly "seeing."

※

Stretch Your Soul
Reverence the smallest of details today, first by noticing, then by drinking in the wonder of their presence on the planet. Allow the "smallest" of creatures to stretch your soul with its perfection and place in the cycle of life.

SPRING IS WHEN YOU FEEL LIKE . . .

Whistling even with a shoe full of mud;
  singing in the pouring rain
with your hair pasted against your forehead;
running through puddles, with sweet abandon, barefoot;
digging into the soil, in spite of the dirt
  caked under your fingernails;
picking flowers and filling your house with them;
hanging sheets outdoors,
  even if you have to wear a jacket and gloves;
planting herbs, even if the ground is too wet;
dancing in and out of your shadow
  as the sun warms your body;
cleaning your windows of the grime and grit of winter;
watching a fat robin enjoy a worm;
opening the windows;
smelling the breeze;
walking;
stopping!

❦

What Does Spring Mean?
Think about what spring means for you and make
your own list. *What happens inside you when new life,
warm breezes, and the soft sounds of spring appear?*

THE TRUTH OF PARADOX

Spring brings to mind the reality of the most paradoxical truth that undergirds all life. *Only in dying can new life come forth. Death **is** the harbinger of life.* Growth in the spiritual life rests on this truth. The contradictions and tensions present in every life are not impediments in the spiritual life, but an integral part of inner growth. Through the paradoxes of life we can learn that the power of life comes not from us alone, but from God—*the Other.*

In the midst of contradiction lies the opportunity to discover grace—a gift to all whose lives are pulled between the poles of paradox. The contradictions experienced in the human journey are a source of insecurity that uncover the source of real security. At every level of our outer and inner lives—work, family and friends—we are stretched and torn between apparently irreconcilable opposites. The way we respond is pivotal to soulful living.

Our only response is to live the contradictions, experience the emotions, and allow the tension to move us deep within to be transformed. This requires a third eye—a spiritual eye that perceives everything as sacred.

🕸

The Harbingers of Spring
Be on the lookout for the paradoxes presented by the harbingers of spring. Allow them to trigger within you the paradoxes in your own life. *What truths have the contradictions taught you? How have these tensions transformed your attitudes and actions?*

GIVING BIRTH TO SELF

The creative juices flowed
  as hormonal levels rose.
She—a woman about to give birth—
    wondered the shape and appearance,
    gender and size of the emerging life within.

These same creative waters merged—mingled,
    blurred—blended
into new forms
shaping purpose
creating new life forms,
    birthing new life in a myriad of mysteries.
She became her real self!

But not without price or pain
    this birthing.
Risk—dare
    Enter—erupt
        Ride the pain, waves of energy
            surging within to discover—
The "I Am" to which each is called
    from the beginning of time.

⅗⅗

Who Am I?
Ponder this: You are . . . *"birthing new life in
a myriad of mysteries."* Then write a short
description of the "I Am" to which you have
been called from the beginning of time.

BALANCING ACT

So, I woke up this morning. . . .
Snow covered the drooping daffodils
for the third time this spring.
My spirit seemed to slink out of grasp,
but I kept to the routine—grind coffee beans—
shower—dress—peruse the paper.
My plans for the day shot down . . .
no planting of the bare root shrub roses—
hope of pink summer blooms—
the motivating image to get me through the day.
No, for me all seemed in upheaval;
a sense of unrest hurled me into confused musings.
I reached for the phone—NO! That's an escape.
Keep busy, clean out that stuffed drawer—
Closets bid my attention—
perhaps if I move some clothes around
I would feel more like spring?
The dreariness of winter's long siege
hovered at my door.
I was sick and tired of its dark clouds and cold winds,
but the day had just begun.
How to regain myself—my center?
There was nothing to do but wrap myself in winter's coat,
gloves and scarf, and lug my half-asleep
body out the door.
As I walked the country road and backyard woods,
I began to notice.

Under the thick wet flakes
    brave spears of peony, blood red,
        thrust through the brown ground;
  purple pansy faces laughed and nodded as I passed;
through the fog of fat flakes I noticed
    a green smear, ever so faint,
washed over boughs and branches of trees and shrubs.
All was not lost—my spirit quickened.
The newness of promised warm winds
    was just around the corner.
See, I am doing something new! Now it springs forth,
  do you not perceive it? (Isaiah 43:19)

What Lifts Up Your Soul?
The energy of the soul brings us to our center; it has
the power to renew our sagging spirits. Today, think
about the smallest things that lift your soul, replacing
your tired spirit with joy. *What is your soul? How
does your inner spirit affect your daily living?*

RAGS

What are rags if not the leftovers of outgrown, outmoded, worn-out clothing? Discarded bits of toweling, underwear, and shirts. Cut off buttons. Cut away the thick seams. Cut down to size for dusting, washing or mopping. Rags are becoming a thing of the past, what with disposable towels, specially treated microfiber cloths and sponges that pop up when wet. They even have rags that pop out of a box! But my grandmother had a penchant for good, clean, sturdy rags. She washed, bleached, dried, and ironed them every week. Tuesday mornings—ironing day—she finished her basketload by pressing flat and folding with care her supply of rags. Rags readied for the spills, dust and dirt of the week to follow.

In the rhythm of her week, rags fit in nicely. I carry on the rag legacy—not to the point of ironing, but I gain a great deal of satisfaction in cutting and tearing rags. Old cotton shirts are best for windows; soft cotton-knit underwear to polish and dust; and old towels are best for drinking up the water sprayed over the just-cleaned car or porch furniture. So much potential in the worn-out shreds of fabric we call rags.

I lament the rolls of paper toweling—so many trees used and tossed into landfills. I am stunned that so many pay for rags, treated and touted with cleaners and toxic formulas to make the art of cleaning easier. Sensitive to the ecology and to voluntary simplicity, I want to promote the return of the humble rag. Rags that cost nothing. Rags that recycle discarded clothing. I am glad I had a grandmother who was so careful with the common rag.

Living More Lightly
Remember stories of how family members who lived through the Great Depression saved and reused simple items that we discard with little thought. *What simple efforts can you make to live more lightly on this planet? What does our modern wastefulness say about our attitudes toward living creation?*

LOVE THE LIFE YOU HAVE, IT'S A BEAUTIFUL ONE

Bankrupt and reduced to the lowest point of his sixty-some years, he had fought off so much—physical pain, cancer and loss. He could stand it no longer so he made plans to end it all. He drove off taking all the pills he could find and several bottles of booze. It felt good to take charge, to be in control of something! Rain battered against the windshield as he drank right out of the vodka bottle. Washing down the pills with alcohol, his mind drifted and the tension split away as darkness began to settle around him. All went black!

He awoke in a ditch in the middle of the night on a deserted road, far from everywhere. Someone was banging on his window. A man, a spirit, or an angel, he wasn't sure. The fuzziness in his head confused his perceptions as he sank further into the black velvet dark womb.

Shaken and scared he awoke once again. This time it was sunlight streaming through a window that startled him awake. Where was he and how did he get there? In a bed, some motel room, who knows where—but—he wasn't dead. Time to finish the job. He looked for a razor, but he hadn't packed his shaving kit. So he broke a glass on the bathroom counter, poised to slip the jagged shard across his wrist. But the mirror caught his attention. He looked at himself, into his own eyes. Eyes that he saw each day in the eyes of his children, his grandchildren. Something about those eyes! Eyes are the windows into the soul. It all happened in a fraction of a second. The flicker of glass made a prism of color as it danced through the sunlit room and bounced against the mirror. The jagged weapon of death fell from his hand as he remembered the precious bits of the life he lived. As he dialed the phone for home, he wondered how he got to this place. He wondered how he could destroy his life. He wondered how he could learn to live again.

⊰⟡⊱

Keep Your Spirit Alive

As you recall those down, depressing moments in life, take up a paper and pen to begin a list of all the wonderful experiences, encounters and people that keep your spirit soaring. Write down a few affirmations—positive qualities about yourself—and place them on index cards. Use these affirmations on depressing days by putting them on your mirror, in your car visor, and in your wallet.

IMAGES AND ICONS

I am haunted by an image that has become an icon of the paradox *death gives way to life.* When the cyclones flooded the African continent in the spring of 2000, Mozambique was turned into an ocean of swirling waters of death. Many sought high ground and refuge in high trees swarming with snakes and stinging insects. The photograph that appeared in American newspapers became a symbol and source of hope. A woman giving birth, high in a tree as a helicopter hovered above, is rescued with her newborn daughter. Amidst all the death and destruction, new life emerges.

So many times this ancient hope is repeated. An aging grandparent dies and a new child is born. Fire destroys all in its path and the phoenix rises out of the ashes, bringing a new sense of what really matters. So many living out their last days in the pain of cancer or other terminal illness learn the lessons of how to really live.

Winter merges into spring as the planet spins. Death brings forth life. The brown branches of the dogwood tree appear dead at first glance. But a closer look reveals the faintest trace of pale green and the knobs of swollen buds. What seemed dead holds the promise of pink flower heads nodding their "yes" in days to come. When I allow myself to enter into images of death I am drawn deep into the recesses of the paradox, lured on by the hope of life. It never fails, for some new thing of beauty and truth is always found in the depths of death.

What Image Haunts You?
Enter into the paradox of death and new life by
seeking an icon in nature, in human relationships,
in the world community. You will know it when
your heart is moved. Allow the image to haunt you
so that you might learn the lessons of hope that are
beyond human understanding.

AFFIRMATIONS

Earth is crammed with heaven,
if we only stop and look.

Children teach us what life is all about through their innocent power of wonder and awe.

In discovering the sacred in ourselves, we learn the language for God.

Live in the moment, for tomorrow is uncertain and yesterday has passed.

To fly we need resistance.

Look up when you are walking, open your hands to another—drink in the ecstasy of life.

In brokenness one can find beauty.

The universe asks for everything we've got. In return she offers more that we knew to ask for.

What matters most is the care of the soul. Even more, the awesome task of guiding the souls of those who come after us is a profound responsibility.

To surrender and admit your powerlessness is to tap into the source of authentic power.

The rainbow after a storm is only seen when there is sunlight. So, too, the grace buried in pain and struggle is unearthed in exposing our suffering to the light of day.

☙❧

Drink Deep of the Spirit
Write these affirmations on note cards or record
them on a tape. Carry them with you for a few days
and reflect upon them, allowing your inner spirit
to drink deeply of their truth.

SLEEPWALKING

Unconscious but alive,
  drugged by the demands to do more,
    to produce more, to accomplish more,
Sleep lost to fit in yet one more
    responsibility—women are losing
    one hour of sleep each night.

Stretched tight in the rubberband
    of earning, pursuing, stressing,
    men repress this pressure to succeed
      until hearts give out and strokes paralyze.

Beauty lies just under the surface of the ordinary,
    yet the ordinary escapes us as we rush about
    accomplishing the empty pit of nothing.
For the really real is not in the doing, but the being;
    not in the acquiring, but in the giving;
    not in the caretaking but in the caregiving.

The blush of life permeates each day.
    Will we embed our lives in
      pursuits that punish and perish . . .
    Or will we choose life?
It only takes a little looking and seeing,
    perceiving and heeding!

❈

Time Out for Life
Release some of your stress by taking time today
to walk, look around and be still. In the stillness we
discover the Source of Life. If you wish, write some
thoughts in your journal or in a letter to yourself.

REVERENCE

Reverence is an inner disposition, an attitude that honors all of life. It is a response filled with wonder and awe at each encounter. As we come into contact with the essence of people, nature, and everything in this vast universe, it gradually dawns on us that all is sacred. It is the only deterrent we as humans have for the violence that rips at the heart of humanity.

The culture encourages us to take rather than give, to compete rather than collaborate, to seek power *over* rather than power *with* one another. In our arrogance we are destroying the lives of children, the balance of the ecosystems, and the promise of justice for the impoverished. Yet we are overwhelmed. What can one person, like me, do to stand up against these waves of destruction? While many are called and gifted to make bold systemic changes in this lust for power, more do not know the path of politics, lobbying and legalese. As with most things, we can only begin by changing ourselves.

We can cultivate a childlike attitude of wonder and awe that honors all life, the cycles of life, and the unfolding of life. Rather than justifying our lack of reverence for the members of the human family that cannot or will not contribute to the common good, we must cultivate a compassion that empowers. Rather than exploit the weaker forms of life with pesticides, hormones, and guns, we must discover the wisdom of nature's balance and order. Rather than hoard our material possessions, our money, and our energy, we must embrace new ways of sharing and separating our needs from our wants. Reverence is a holy perception that understands all of creation as significant and profoundly important in the web of life.

୫◊୫

Harmony from Reverence

Think deeply about the value of life each day. Stand in awe before the least created being and learn from its cycle of life. Develop a reverence for each person you meet to bring about the harmony we all desire. *How can you begin your day with this attitude? What reminders can you use to trigger your resolve to become more reverent?*

SUNRISE

Sun streamed with an almost
unbearable light—
  rays bounced against the kitchen window
my shadow clearly defined
  now on the refrigerator
  then across the counter
      as I poured a cup of coffee.
The birth of the sun
  on a long-awaited, long-anticipated spring day,
  forgets my mind
      winter's dark bleak
lightless dronings—on and on.
I am alive
  with light. Energy sparks
  flow from fingers
      in the waters that rinse the cup and spoon.
I am alive
  with hearing bird song
  as I crack open paned glass
      for a deep silent breath.
I am alive with sun's light
  that dances my heart, lightens my gait,
      and soars my soul
to heights of heaven sent rising.
Now ears and heart and soul awaken
  I see your light!

Come into the Light

It is in the pause between tasks that we come alive.
Stop several times today to discover what the light
reveals to you in silent stopping. Write your own
poem or thoughts about coming alive.

JUDY'S CHALLENGE

Eighty or more teenagers sat on the floor singing and sharing their thoughts on God's presence in their lives when she entered the room. As she clomped over everyone to get to the place closest to the group's leader, the conversation was punctuated by her heavy step and her words of greeting to everyone she knew. That was our Judy. Mentally and physically challenged from birth, she produced chaos and disarray wherever she went.

While on the surface she seemed a disruptive presence, the eighteen-year-old began to transform the sophisticated airs of these upper-middle-class adolescents. She had a clumsy bear hug for everyone, refreshing among the self-restrained, self-conscious youth. Judy labored to be understood as she tried to share her spiritual life, just like the others. While her speech was not distinct, if you listened carefully, her wisdom and innocence were profound.

Garrulous and noisy, Judy became the friend of many as they learned the lessons of patience, compassion and reverence for life. Virulent, handsome football players helped Judy over ruts and hills as she tried to keep up with the group on a hiking expedition. The girls included Judy, teaching her dance steps to the latest popular songs. Her thank-you came in the form of hand-painted pictures filled with childlike figures of people holding hands in a circle. There were so many things she contributed to the spirit of the group by her presence. Judy, the challenged one, challenged us all to look deeply into the essence of the person, rather than stopping at the physical surface of appearances.

Judy was the source of an invaluable lesson for adolescents forming a sense of real identity. What would have happened if Judy had not had the encouragement of her parents to join the group? What would have happened if Judy had not been born?

⣎⣿⣵

From the Least among You

Notice the way in which you are influenced by outward appearances as you travel through the course of this day—this week. Risk venturing further to discover the gifts of each human person, in spite of how they look or act. *How do you view the mentally and physically challenged? What gifts have you found in the least expected persons and experiences?*

THE DANCE

In the stillness of your soul, reflect upon the sacredness of your life, of all life. Relax. Find a place where you will not be interrupted. Quiet your inner voice and any distracting thoughts. Become one with the beat of your heart and each breath.

Begin by thinking about the crucible-womb of the cosmos that holds the human family and all of creation under her breasts. Therein lies the potential to consciously continue the growth—the becoming and creating of a new heaven and a new earth. *What feelings emerge as I think about being held in the womb of the cosmos?*

Imagine the ordered movement of the planets, the galaxies, and the many universes. This is the most primitive liturgy, the cosmic dance. It is not a random or chaotic dance, but one that is ordered, fluid, and filled with wonder. All of humanity participates in this dance of the universe. In fact, we are each a microcosm of the universal dance, unraveling our potential, in a tapestry of bright colors over all that is. *Can I risk joining in the dance of the universe by offering my gifts for the good of all of creation?*

Allow your thought to turn to the Source of Life. Embedded deep within the womb of the universe is a higher power many call "God." Continually creating and bringing everything to fullness, the Creator permeates all life. *What are my images of the Divine? How would I describe the Source of Life?*

Focus your reflection upon yourself. Remember those times you experienced a nagging sense that *there is something more I was born to do—to be.* This is the longing to discover one's true vocation in life. To become, to fulfill our human potential, to find meaning in the work of our hands, to create with the Author of Life itself, is essential for the cosmic dance to continue.

This process begins in the silent stillness of self-discovery of our uniqueness, our gifts, and our bliss. In the inner dialogue, ask yourself: *What gives me life—energy? What opens me to love? Where do I find passion? What drains me—saps the life out of me? What blocks me or holds me back from life and love?*

When we discover our gifts, our passion for life, and our hidden treasure, we discover we are already dancing— swaying and tapping our toes to the rhythms of the universe. Joy, love and self-giving will follow. This is our mission in life, this self-discovery process and the following of order of the planets and stars that have guided humankind for generations. We cannot worry about taking the wrong steps or allow the risk of looking like a fool to keep us out of the dance. We will never experience the joy and wonder of the energy that ebbs and flows through and around each particle of creation if we do not dare to dance. We will never bring about the fullness of life if we fail to discover our unique contribution to this wonderful and wild universe. We will not create a universe of harmony, peace and justice if we refuse to risk offering our gifts to the cosmos.

⁂

Out of the Depths
Think about the gifts that you have unearthed from the depths of your being. Name them and claim them.

HANDS

Pudgy, soft and tiny,
  Ryan's hands coil around my finger;
caught in his grasp the sun-spotted wrinkled hands
    are work-worn from gardening and sewing,
while his milk-white smooth skinned
    hands tingle with sensations of first-felt
        textures and shapes.
Poised in a game of clapping, Elizabeth's hands
    extended by four years of growth to grasp her violin,
touch her mother's slender curved
    palms in a moment of exuberant joy.

Hands that comfort, touch, love, and caress,
    learn, discover, explore, and create.
Of every size and shape, bruised and callused,
smooth and refined, hands hold
    the stories of lifetimes
        of generations
            of the legacy
    that all humans need to touch and be touched.
Hands move the human adventure forward,
express emotions that have no words,
    have a language all their own.

※

Hands-on Nurturing
Think about the hands that have nurtured you—your
hands nurturing others. *How do you express your
inner self with your hands? What do you pass on to
the next generation through the gift of your hands?*

Regeneration

Walls hold, contain, enclose.
Keeping secrets:
scenes of lovemaking
warring dinner tables
sad silences of solitude
moments of "ah ha!"
Holding memories:
celebrations marking years of
raucous, tipsy times
bedtime rituals and morning routines
tearful times and times of "hooray!"
The walls' embrace is the caress called home.
Protection against the outside storms
that sometimes seep through pours and cracks,
walls hold families together.
Walls burn down,
or are destroyed,
or are abandoned for newer and better walls
or the walls of a nursing home or hospital
or the walls of a casket.
I wonder who is listening
as the walls tell their stories over and over again.

❦

Living Memories
Recall the homes you have lived in and the
memories that those walls contain. *What
memories remain alive within you that you might
pass on to future generations?* You might choose
to write these down or record them in some way.

THE JOLT INTO REALITY

From time to time our perspective is renewed and the value of life is underlined. These moments of intense awareness offer an opportunity for the spirit to realign with what really matters. Such was the case with a young family who had made it financially and, thus, materially.

Their new home was replete with every possible modern convenience from Jacuzzi to master suite and from large airy rooms on the living floor to lovely gardens outdoors. Material things were important to them as they had worked hard and saved carefully to gain their treasured possessions. Living the good life, far beyond the American dream, became their reality.

All that suddenly shrank to insignificance when their gas grill exploded and their house caught on fire. The custom kitchen with the latest in modern conveniences became ash, lumps of melted metal, and scorched wood in a matter of minutes. The huge walk-in closet above was a burned-out room in which hung empty hangers and the remnants of storage boxes. Everything was smoke and soot.

During the months it took to clean and rebuild, the family repeatedly expressed their gratitude that no one was injured when the grill blew, that they got their children out before the fire spread and trapped them, and that they had family, neighbors and friends to help them deal with their losses. The expensive mural painted on the crumpled kitchen wall, the new appliances, and the lovely new drapes never caused major concern, so great was their gratitude for not losing the lives of those they loved. While we live materially in a consumer-driven world, the importance of life and love are never far from the human capacity to be more.

❧

I Am Grateful for . . .
As you think about this story and those moments in your own life where your values were jarred into the proper perspective, make a list of those people for whom you are grateful. Then take the time to tell them.

THE COST OF FREEDOM

One speculates, standing on Omaha Beach in Normandy, France: What would the world be like if the young men had not had the courage to plow through the waters and scale the chalk-white cliffs against impossible odds? What if the generals did not have the vision to risk it all against tanks, concrete bunkers and scores of enemy troops? What if one general had not left his troops to celebrate his wife's birthday? What if . . . ?

As the wind cut through my raincoat and a fine mist blew against my cheeks on that beach, I wondered about the price paid for freedom. Like a television camera, my mind swept through more recent images of war: a girl child running down a road in Vietnam, naked flesh burned by napalm; missiles lighting up the night sky in the Persian Gulf; heaps of bodies buried in shallow graves in Bosnia; and villagers in Africa caught in a crossfire of guerrilla fighters. Weighed down in a deep sadness, I weep for the young men who died on D day, for we seem to have squandered the freedom won in the rain of blood. They gave it all so that every human person would be valued. Nations offered their best on the altar of war so that all races and religions would be equal. When will we learn the lesson these men and women taught us in the prime of their youth? Have they been lost only to be remembered, ever so slightly, almost trivially, one day each year?

Name Your Demons
Move deep within to discover ways in which
you are not free, ways in which you do not honor
the freedom of others. Discover your hidden prejudices. Name them, either by speaking them aloud
or writing them in your journal. Once the demons
are named, you can begin to change little behaviors
that disempower others.

SPRING STORMS

Lightning cut the night sky
as wind howled and thunder roared.
The rain pelted my windshield.
   I held the steering wheel in white-knuckled fear.
Raw fear is primordial!
The two-lane country roads were awash in pools
   of wind-blown water.
I could barely see my street as
   hailstones drove into the car,
      punctuating my hammering heart
      in that night's terror.
It was when I pulled into my driveway,
   breathing a prayer of thanks,
      that the tension eased out of my rigid body.

Oh, the morning's light brought
   a calm, sunlit greenness to everything.
(The ozone in the electrical flashes.)
Of course, spring storms are welcome for the
   needed rain and growing of things,
but as I wandered around the yard piling
   tree limbs into my wheelbarrow,
the fear of the night before
   shot through me
and I understood the power of nature
   once again and contemplated my own smallness
      in the order of things.

The Perspective of Nature

Remember your own experiences when the power of nature put perspective on your position in this vast universe. *What lessons about life can you learn from this realization? How does nature's power help you keep your perspective?*

A SPRING SPIRIT

Birdsong is listened for each morning
until the squawk of the blue jay
    can be distinguished from the warning chirp
        of the robin guarding her nest.
Middle-aged couples walking hand in hand
    bring a nostalgic longing for the springtime of love.
All is readied—becoming new, shining and cleaned
    in the order and organization of spring-cleaning.
Looking close you revel in the hues of white
    magnolia, azalea, snowdrops, verbena,
            lilies-of-the-valley,
        and wands of drooping spirea.
Nesting birds, torrents of rain,
        green glory high on magnificent trees
    texture your spirit, titillating every sense.
Arms are bared to the warm sun and breezes
    as you open your soul to a world alive
        and astir with growing.
Listen to the language of the flower
    as it speaks in nodding grace.
Tune your soul to the sun's rising
    and setting in magnificent golds and reds.
Allow the music of spring
    to enter your cells and sinews:
    creating, transforming and revitalizing you
        with a swallow of spring
    with each moment's wonder.

Welcome to the Spirit of Spring

Imbue your spirit with the season of spring. Allow this season to take hold of you for a day or even a moment. Take time at the end of the day to name the transforming effect this season has had upon your spirit.

OF GARDENING AND PAST GENERATIONS

As I plant the seeds of bush beans and stop to admire the lovely lettuce leaves of chartreuse, burgundy and deep green, I realize how life-giving gardening has been in my life. Whenever I feel the tension of the day rise up along the back of my neck I can go out and pull a few weeds or plant a tomato or cabbage seedling and forget the troubles of the day. Handfuls of dirt, through my fingers and under my nails, are a lifeline, a point of connection to something bigger, to something more.

This legacy was passed to me by my maternal grandmother, who had a postage-sized yard, full of garden. She did not limit her plot to vegetables, but spilling over the edges of every piece of brown dirt were old roses, portulaca, hosta, and dianthus. She would patiently help me place the tiny carrot and lettuce seeds into small trenches she traced in the soil with her finger. She taught me the difference between cabbage and kohlrabi, parsley and parsnips. Side by side we would hunt the dark earth for potatoes and beets. Her garden was an orderly array of bounty.

I remember those moments of intimacy with my grandmother today as I look at her old white and green hostas growing along the border of my vegetable patch. As I bend over the soil, guiding the tiny hands of my own granddaughter, she drops tiny seeds into my traced trenches. I know I am passing on a gift—the love of life and the utter freshness of living things to her.

❦

What Is Your Legacy?
Think about the gifts passed on to you by past generations of people who cared for you. *What memories are triggered, what legacy do you still carry? How can you pass this legacy to the next generation?*

NAMING THE SACRED

Try this ritual to celebrate the sacredness of all life.

⸙⸙ To Prepare

Gather several reminders of new life from nature that catch your eye as you take a spring walk. Look through a photo album and select a few pictures of people you reverence. Finally, choose a few items in your home that have special significance for you. Find a quiet place where you will not be interrupted. Light a candle, burn some incense, or dim the lights to create a mood of rest and quiet.

⸙⸙ The Ritual

Once you are comfortable, quiet your mind and heart by breathing deeply and erasing any worries from your consciousness. Enter the depths of your being and the silence of your spirit. When you are ready, select one of the objects you have gathered and look at it. Study the surface . . . the color, texture, smell, and shape. Then move beyond the surface into the essence of the object. *What makes it what it is? Wherein lies its beauty and appeal for you? What lessons about life does it speak to your inner being?* With reverence lift the object high above your head in a gesture of thankfulness, pausing for a moment, and place it in front of you near the candle. Do this with several objects. Repeat the process for the photos of the people you chose. Reflect upon the giftedness of each person, their significance in your life, connections they might have to your soul.

When you have finished, close this ritual with a prayer or conversation with the Source of All Life. You might also express the emotions you experienced in this ritual by writing in your journal or composing a poem.

Summer

Introduction

We live in a compartmentalized world. Therefore, the natural tendency toward unity and wholeness is thwarted by the distractions of daily survival. All day long we switch hats, from working person, spouse, parent, friend, neighbor, and companion. From childhood on we learn and collect images of what these roles look like in outward appearances, attitudes, and behaviors. No wonder we are stressed. No wonder it is hard to sift through the range of roles to discover our real self. Even more difficult is the primary life's work of discovering the inner self. But, without the discovery and reintegration of our compartmentalized living into a seamless whole we will never find the authentic spirit that motivates our being and gives purpose to our living.

Summer is a season for rediscovering the art of holistic living. Recovering not merely the union of our complicated personhood, but also the unity of all of life. We are created in union with all of creation and the Creator. We do not choose community, that is, communion with others and the created in the universe, we are already one. Life is a journey toward recovering that original intended unity. Until we rediscover what we already are, we will not find that still-point of the spirit that will refresh our soul.

This lifelong pursuit of wholeness is like the quest for the Holy Grail. The search for the Holy Grail captured the imagination of humans for centuries in the past. In recent decades, the excitement of space travel and the possibility of visiting the moon and the other planets of our galaxy became the focus of speculation. When we saw ourselves from space and realized how beautiful this planet is, we came to understand how connected we are to one another and all of the created cosmos.

Today, the human imagination is caught in the wonder of exploring inner space. What lies buried within the human potential for creating and companioning? How can we mine these rich treasures and pass them to succeeding generations, empowering them for life and love? As we move inward, with the gift of intuition to map the journey, we will discover that we are indeed capable of deep communion.

WONDERS WITHIN

Rosebud wrapped tight in velvet petals
   guards fragrant future seeds of life;
Cocooned in taut, silky thread
   protected pupa suspends in time to emerging butterfly;
Coiled fetal life in warm womb waters
   holds wonder in miniature human form.

What wonders do we hold
   within soul's depths?
Wherein do our wings bring life
   to fan the toiling of human hands?
Where do hearts flee in life's mixed
   journeying to joy and jaded dreams?

Dwelling within coiled, wrapped human flesh and bones
   imagination dreams,
      spirit soars,
         passion surges,
   sensation stirs—
   we rumble with the awakening truth
      and dawning reality—
Within the human person dwells the living God,
   the treasure trove of our quest.

※

What Wonders I Hold
Take a few moments to look deep within yourself
and make a list of the qualities you possess, asking:
What wonders do I hold within my soul's depths?

BURSTING WITH LIFE

She exudes joy. My friend, Toni, is full of life. I wonder where she gets her energy. I can be that way sometimes, but then my energy fades and I succumb to the dreary dredges of exhaustion. I flail about wondering why I am here and what my purpose is in this life. I realize that in these times I am off center—out of kilter. I accomplish and create with no heed to the nagging need to back off and be still. It is all about centering, she reminds me. Going to the still-point within and seeking my real self.

I think about the wonderful flower—the daylily. Yellow petals open wide to the sun for one full day, then fade and fold. Her beauty seems to fade—her time in the sun complete. But then the real purpose of the daylily begins—forming the fruit for future generations of flowers. I forget to fold my petals—to yield to the rhythms of my body-spirit life. Instead I forge ahead and try to keep open to the sun yet another day. I forget the fruiting, birthing movement in the dark womb of my spirit. The necessary stilling of my heart is fertile soil for future flowering.

I know with all my being that I cannot bear fruit without that still standing in silent awe.

❦

Be Still, My Heart
Allow this image to filter into your depths throughout this day: *"The necessary stilling of my heart is fertile soil for future flowering."*

GRASS

The scent, sweet and spicy,
  fills my head in a delirium of sentimentality,
    as I drive past the newly mowed grass.
It takes me back to Grandfather
    with his hand mower, cutting the postage-stamp lawn
      in front of the old homestead.
His kindness flows through me as I breathe deeply,
    gulping in the aromatic purity of sweet grass.
His solid spirit ripples through my being.
Quiet, serene and secure
    are the memories of a man whose vein-roped arms
      told the toil of hard work in the Ford factory.
Jet black eyes that pierced your soul
    as you stammered to tell the
      truth of some misdeed to a soul so firm.
He was my compass in times of turmoil,
    my rock of refuge in the suffering
      of childhood disappointments,
      my listening post when everyone else was too busy.
A grandfather like that is assurance that God is
    and all will be well.

❦

From Scents to Sentiments
As you breathe in the scents of summer, notice
what happens on the inside—the emotions,
memories and feelings that are triggered by
the sense of smell. *What scents stimulate past
memories that connect you to family and friends?*

THE BOX

I can still vividly recall the day the large box arrived at our house. I was just a girl of six or seven, but even now I can recapture the excitement of the prospects of what lay within, wrapped in the tissue paper of that magical moment. Because we were poor, I wore the hand-me-down clothing of my mother's wealthy customers' children. Ill-fitting clothes readjusted and resized by her talented needle. My child's heart longed for something yellow and instead tried to be happy with the ugliest green garment. But this time, this time there was the sparkle of some new possibility.

I had been waiting for this summer's package of hand-me-downs to arrive. But this was definitely something new—the "Best and Company" label on the box made that certain. Grandmother sternly instructed me to wait until Mom got home from work to open the box. All day long my eyes wandered to the box—the container enclosed new possibilities and hidden treasures. I allowed myself the luxury of imagining how I would look arrayed in all the colors of the rainbow. The possibilities for dresses, shorts and tops were endless. But then I'd stop myself. What if these were just the same old hand-me-downs, wrapped in a new store box? Would I be disappointed with what lay within?

Finally, the great moment arrived—Mom came home! Even before dinner, we opened the box together. Grandpa pulled out his pocketknife to slice through the tape that secured the contents. I trembled as the lid slid off. Will I be disappointed? Will there be a treasure within? Carefully, my mom began to roll back the layers of tissue paper and there were new clothes. Summer shorts and matching tops in yellow and blue. Even a navy skirt with big white buttons down each side. Beautiful colors and clothes and all of them tagged in their crisp newness. We had a fashion show and everything fit as I modeled one outfit after another. It was wonderful to be the first to wear these garments, chosen just for me. What a generous and thoughtful lady, this customer who realized every child needs something new and bright.

Wrapped in the tissue paper of our inner spirit, there are no hand-me-downs. No worn and faded garments lie within, for we are arrayed in unique and wonderful apparel. Tailored to each human heart, the inner spirit fits each of us perfectly and exclusively.

ॐ

One Inner Spirit, Tailored to Fit

Think about all those people who have mentored you into the realization that you are unique. What flows from within as you turn this phrase around in your imagination, *"Tailored to each human heart, the inner spirit fits each of us perfectly and exclusively"*?

IT TAKES A VILLAGE

I was shaped in an inner-city ethnic neighborhood of crowded houses. Neighbors looked out for the bands of ragtag kids that played "cowboys and cowgirls" in the only green spot at the end of the street—the vacant lot. Cars slowed down as we filed back to the sidewalk, interrupting our softball games in the only spot large enough to hold three paper-sack bases—the street. My best friend Barbara's grandmother taught me to make Hungarian *polichintas*. I clung to the back of the ice truck with all the other neighborhood kids. We waited with anticipation for the "paper-rags" man to come down the street. It was especially fun to feed his horse wormy apples. With regularity, the boredom of hot summer days was broken with the arrival of the fruit man, fish man, milkman, and the ice cream truck. While the sun rarely got through the thick tree-crowned, narrow street to burn our skin and there simply was no room to learn to ride a two-wheeler, we enjoyed the contentment of a simpler adolescence.

There were no baby-sitters, since everyone lived in a duplex with grandparents or maiden aunts upstairs or downstairs. No one had to worry about safety since a stranger was immediately recognized. There was always a relative around to walk you the two blocks to school. When we were older we made the journey four times a day (we ate lunch at home) in ganglike groups that would scare away any predator. No one could afford summer camp—I never even heard of such a thing—so we had plentiful playmates throughout the summer months. No expensive toys prevented our creative spirits from soaring, imagining games from the ten-cent movies we watched together every Saturday.

Because of the connections with these neighbors and in spite of the poverty of material things and lack of space, we all grew up valuing family and neighbors. We learned compassion through the care neighbors had for those who were ill or in financial trouble. There was always extra soup in the pot and a nut roll freshly baked to thank someone for a favor. In this tiny neighborhood village we learned the value of an education from folks who could barely speak English. My values and ideals were shaped by immigrants who were more than neighbors. They were my extended family.

☙❧

Name Your Mentors
Remember your early years to discover the connections that shaped and formed your values. Name some of the people who taught you right from wrong and molded your inner spirit. *As you prepare to rest tonight, give thanks for your extended family.*

THE BABY BROTHER

There is a story of a young family preparing a four-year-old girl for the birth of her baby brother. Being a modern family and informed couple, the parents read her stories of siblings, got her a boy doll, and constantly reminded her that she was wonderful and loved. Yet they worried when they brought the baby home from the hospital, for their little girl had been the center of their universe for four long years. They fretted about her reaction to the little one.

When the girl asked to get into the crib and talk to her baby brother—*alone*—the parents were alarmed. They wondered what she might do to the baby. But the toddler insisted that she talk to the baby all by herself. Reminding the four-year-old that she needed to be careful, they turned up the baby monitor and peeked through the nursery door.

What they saw and heard astounded them. The child climbed into the crib, and softly stroked the baby's cheek. As the tiny infant looked up at her big sister, the little girl said, *"Tell me what it is like, where you came from, I am already starting to forget."*

❦

Unlock the Door to Your Spirit Place
The place from which we came and to which we are going is a spirit place, where all is one. Babies hold a key into that dimension of being. Yet the influences of the world distract and block out that memory. Go back to your earliest memories and unlock the door to your inner landscape. *What do you discover about the unity of all things?*

COMMUNION

All cries out in me to be connected:
to see and suffer myself
 in all beings, joined at last.
This thrust from the root of my being
 comes over me from time to time
  like a variable star shooting off its light.
This burning begins and rumbles through every cell:
 Like the opening of petals
  on a time-lapsed flower;
 the wind shearing across tall grass;
 the splitting crack of lightning across an eel green sky.
Hurry down into the black folds
 where earth spins,
  the vortex where the fire begins.
 Let it enfold you, embrace you,
  encompass you in the mellow pools
   swirling upon a pond of collective drops
   of primordial being.

༄

What Do You Risk When You Connect?
Think about a time when you felt this need
to be connected. Use some images to describe
this longing. *What do you risk when you move
into the Source and Center of All Life?*

RECYCLING

Long before it was fashionable, I began to recycle—newspapers and cans, plastic and glass. I even had a compost heap for kitchen scraps and yard waste. But when we moved to the country and had to pay for waste pickup, I was upset to discover that the company we hired to pick up the trash found recycling too expensive. Then my search began.

The bad news turned to renewed excitement. I found a drop-off location about fifteen minutes from my home that not only took the common recyclable items, but also collected magazines and catalogues and, to my surprise, cardboard. I immediately began to sort the numerous catalogues and the cardboard boxes from the regular trash, along with the cans, bottles and newspapers.

You can imagine the heap of stuff that accumulated in the garage as I happily separated the garbage. My husband thought I was nuts and got annoyed when he pulled his car into the garage and couldn't open the door because the reusable waste was in the way. I know there were times on garbage day when he secretly threw the recycled items into the regular garbage late at night.

I learned a lesson from this enthusiasm for saving the earth in my own small way. As long as someone else picked up the recyclables, I had no problem sorting. But when I had to make the effort to load the car with the separated items and drive to the lot where the bins were located, my enthusiasm died down. Since the location was only open during the week, I couldn't nag my husband to take care of this unsavory task. I discovered that talking about the importance of caring for the environment was no problem. I could become animated and passionate about it at a party or giving a retreat. Even the simple task of sorting things was not too difficult. After all, what's the difference between throwing something into a trash can or a recycling bin? But when it came to inconveniencing my schedule or making the extra effort to load the car, drive fifteen minutes out of my way, and throw the trash into the appropriate bins, that was a different story. Isn't it interesting that important things require that something extra?

•••

Connect to the Earth

Reflect upon your experiences at saving the environment. You may choose to list some positive and negative practices you have tried in the past. *What extra effort does it take to live out your values regarding your connection to the earth?*

DISCONNECTION IS DESTROYING US

From our earliest days, the basic connections we have to all of life are fragmented. Blinded by a mechanistic view of humankind, we value usefulness and accomplishment as a criteria for success. Thus, we are driven to live our days on a freeway of rushing, doing and accumulating. With no time to journey the landscape of our inner being, we slowly kill off our authentic potential and deplete our resources. In essence we become the robots we deplore. Isolated, we tout the slogans of rugged individualism. "I'll do it my way. I am a rock, and I can make it on my own." Ultimately, we forget the circle of life and blind our vision to the web that connects everything to the Ultimate Spirit.

Ours is not the fate of mere survival. We have been claimed for something more. The meaning of existence is found only in love. The hierarchical attitudes that require us to step over other beings to climb the ladder to success must undergo a major change. The concept of dualism that separates our very beings into compartments called body and spirit must be transformed. We mistakenly think that we exist first as isolated individuals who could choose to form selective relationships. But, instead, we must come to understand that we are part of a great circle that holds all that exists. Even quantum physics reminds us that nothing exists in itself, but only in relation to something else. What happens to one part of this sacred circle affects the whole and even the smallest part of it. When we restore our severed links within ourselves and with all of creation our lives will be healed and made whole. We will increase our capacity for giving and receiving love. Our acts of love will live on after us and continue to affect the course of human history.

§◊§

What Causes You to Feel Disconnected?
Think about those parts of your life that are most fragmented. *What are the root causes of this sense of isolation and disconnection?* Also, take the time to recall moments and relationships in which you feel a deep sense of connection. *What helps you to feel connected, both within your self and with other creatures?* Resolve to spend quality time on replacing the causes of disconnection with those experiences that bring you a sense of union.

ENVY

It wasn't until adulthood that I realized I harbored jealousy toward one of my brothers. Envy kept me at a distance from him. It's not that we didn't speak or do family things together, but we never seemed to relate. Our blood connection was broken by my own feelings that he somehow got the better end of the deal.

In looking back over our lives together, I realized that I was jealous of him from our childhood days. When he was an infant, we shared the same bedroom in our two-bedroom, rented apartment. That was until he was around the toddler stage and I would wake him when I got ready for bed. Since I was already eight years old, my bedtime was an hour later than his. I was moved downstairs to my grandmother's apartment, where she had an extra bedroom off her kitchen. But I suffered through terrifying nights in that little room, for Grandma would watch the only television upstairs in my parents' apartment and Grandpa worked nights. I was frightened and alone.

This sense of abandonment continued when Gary moved into our new home with my parents and I stayed with my grandparents to finish out the school year. I still feel the ache of longing to live in the long-anticipated new house today. While none of these experiences were my brother's doing, I must have carried the feelings of envy with me right into adulthood. Once I could name the feelings, embrace them, and examine their origins, I could let go of the jealousy that severed my connection with Gary. While we are very different people, I can now enjoy his tales of fishing and hunting and deeply admire his patience and skill in working with mentally challenged adults. In letting go of envy, I could recover a tie with a family member who gifts my life.

§◊§

What Consumes You?
We often desire the life or the gifts possessed by another. Envy can consume our thoughts and contort our behaviors. As you think about the constraints envy has had in your life seek the origins of the jealousy you carry. *What can you do today to let go and become free to relate to and communicate with those you envy?*

ORIGINAL SIN

I know a brokenness exists in the human spirit
when the spilt milk all over the fresh tablecloth
and down my son's cast, making it squishy, sets me off.
I speak harshly at the little one, whose
lower lip quivers—I ignore her in my raving mood—
and slam out the door, forgetting my purse
and the gas tank is on empty—
darn those teenage drivers!—
so I curse at the driver slowly making a right turn,
wondering if I will make it to work.
The phone's interruptions annoy me and I don't even
notice my secretary's new hairdo, finding it hard
to concentrate on the report due in fifteen minutes.
The litany of my broken day drones on until lunchtime.
With resolve I decide I need a breath of air,
as I flee the office for a fast-paced walk.
Concentrating, huffing, angry, I bump into a
little old woman selling carnations for cancer research.
Her proffered fist holds a white one in my face.
A bark of a "no" raises in my throat
and I stop dead in my tracks.
My little one loves white carnations—an offering
to heal the split of spilt milk.

%%

Heal the Rift
Try noticing how one small disaster can spew into your
whole day. *What causes you to disconnect? How can
you heal the rift that creeps into your daily relationships?*

ON FORGIVENESS

Not forgetting or denying,
  condoning or excusing,
but responding to injustice
    free of resentment or revenge.
Hard not to take a morally superior stance
    in the face of being wronged.
Difficult to hold in prayer;
    impossible to love with a largeness of heart,
        one so deserving of disdain.
But forgiveness freely chosen
    frees the spirit to soar
        over the locked gates around a wronged soul.
Opening to healing, forgiveness,
    transforms a life for more!

❦

Open Your Heart
Think about the emotional toil on your body and
spirit when you hold back forgiveness. *What steps
can you take to open your heart to healing? How can
you let go of resentment?*

LETTING GO

Take some time to try this spiritual exercise on forgiveness. Find a place where you will not be disturbed. Into that place take some objects that you find soothing—a candle, a favorite pillow or covering, a photo or painting, and something from nature. Let your body relax as your senses take in your comfort items. Think about why they bring you ease.

When you are ready, close your eyes and become aware of your breathing. Your heartbeat. Relax and sink down into the deepest level of your spirit—your truest self. Know that in this place you are not alone. The Spirit of the Universe—God—is your guide.

At an appropriate time, think about a person who has hurt you, either in the past or more recently. Allow that person to emerge without any effort on your part. Go back to that moment of pain or injustice and immerse yourself in the feelings evoked within your spirit. You may find that tears fill your eyes, anger and even rage floods your heart, and revenge lurks in the recesses of your soul. Allow these feelings free reign.

Notice how your body changes when you experience these feelings. What happens to your muscles, your heartbeat, your breathing? Know, in the deepest part of yourself, that this inability to forgive takes a physical as well as a spiritual toll on your personhood.

Now look deeply into the eyes of the person who wronged you. See in him/her the goodness that the Creator placed into the soul and heart of this person. If you cannot find the goodness, it is enough to know that a tiny fleck of it is buried within his/her spirit.

As you continue this healing process, you find you are in a small room with a window. The room is filled with balloons. After a time of confusion, you realize that these balloons are waiting for you to free them. Attached to each balloon is a blank card. On the cards, imagine yourself writing the feelings and thoughts that you long to set free as you seek to forgive this person. Spend time now ridding your spirit of whatever comes to mind as you make the effort to forgive. Simply write down the thought and let the balloon out of the window.

When you are ready, you can leave the room, knowing that you can return any time. Know too that the Spirit will guide you through the difficult process of forgiveness.

⁂

Freedom to Forgive
Repeat this meditation whenever you are
held back or blocked from loving. The goodness
that is God fills each open heart.

WHAT REAL FREEDOM MEANS

When I first met Ella, she was obsessed with her looks and her body. A large woman, she camouflaged it well with the cut of designer clothes that flattered. Ella bought tons of clothes to make sure she and her family, including five children, looked like they dressed out of the latest fashion catalogue. Whenever she got bored she would redecorate another room. I thought she was a superficial person.

After many years of casual encounters where we talked about the toils of raising children, decorating the rooms of our homes, and the latest quick and easy recipes, Ella spilled out her secret to me over coffee. She had never told anyone, including her husband, that as a young girl she had been sexually molested by a man she trusted. Ella could not hold back the flood of fear and anger any longer. She confessed that she never enjoyed sex in her marriage and feared her spouse would have an affair or, worse still, leave her.

Twenty-five years of hiding this secret damaged her health, her marriage and her self-image. Once Ella could reveal her secret and name the injustice committed against her, she could begin the healing process. With therapy, she emerged as a full woman, no longer bored and addicted to shopping. She lost weight, and the worry lines, once covered by heavy makeup, have melted into a special glow and beauty from within. Ella no longer worries about what people think about her or her family, particularly regarding clothes—their outward appearances.

When I asked her how she came to free her spirit and forgive the abuser, she simply said, *"You just put one foot in front of the other. Begin with small steps. The first one is admitting to someone that you have been unjustly harmed and realizing that you need not be ashamed."* We have become close friends ever since that day over coffee.

❦

Be Honest with Yourself
We all carry secrets. Sometimes we feel shame that another has treated us in an unjust way. Today, take the time to be more honest with yourself and uncover your secret resentments. *What small step can you take to begin the process of healing?*

CAUGHT IN THE CLUTCHES OF FEAR

Break open our blocked caves
to help us find each other;
Release the heart to act in love.
Caved in,
    Caved heart,
        Drapes drawn,
            Doors locked,
                Security systems in place.
Safe in shrouded silence,
  isolated in neighborhoods,
locked tight against fear.
A mother, a son, a dog,
  dead thirty days before
    anyone noticed.
  Found by a postal carrier who noticed
    piled-up mail.
Frozen forms—
  shapeless—faceless—
All cry out against the
  impersonal techno culture.
A woman is stabbed repeatedly
  while sealed windowed buildings
  silenced the sounds of her
    cries for help.
If anyone heard
  no one wanted to get involved.

This is a disgrace on a nation
  numbed by disenchanted dysfunction
    media-hype to sell news.
Transform, transcend
  flying windows open.
Crack open our fear,
  broaden our horizons to care,
    to carry concern
      in compassionate confidence
  against the wall of fear.
Sweep our streets
  with tornadic winds of change,
    shattering glass, locks and bars.
Release us from fright and panic;
  revision us to see the heart of
  the other—
    soul of each sister,
      of each brother.

༄

Loosen the Grip of Fear
What fears cause you to close your eyes, heart and soul to others? Name and trace the hold those fears have on your heart. Only then can you release them to the winds of change.

BREAKING UP A HOME

There was much to do to prepare my husband's childhood home for sale. With both of his parents dead, it fell to us to sell the contents and the house. But for us it was not just applying the coats of paint, replacing the broken window-panes, or emptying the cupboards and closets. Instead, we took great care with the treasures that held this family of origin together.

I clearly remember the spices and the cookbooks. As I sorted and arranged them for the house sale my mind paused to reminisce about the wonderful cakes and cookies my mother-in-law baked for family dinners and holidays. As I picked up a tin of cinnamon, I felt a wave of nostalgia, for her cinnamon buns were a work of art. I simply could not throw the tin into the trash. Long empty of its contents, the container has followed me through the years and even on our move to a new home. My cupboards still hold the turn-of-the-century cookbook, with pages stained from egg whites and cocoa, butter and vanilla. Her fingerprints remain in the leaves that have long since separated from the book's binding.

The dining room table and chairs that my father-in-law worked overtime to purchase remain to this day in my kitchen, a hub around which many family meals have been shared. Even when the veneer was burned in our house fire, we had a refinisher shave off the burned surface of the tabletop so we could keep the memory of our connection to these two who died so young. In fact, we still use the Ethan Allen bedroom set that we did not have the heart to sell. In the end there was little in that house sale, for their home held too many treasures. At my sister-in-law's home, we still eat off her mother's china, and I wear her original wedding ring next to my own. All that was left was a shell of a house. But we are enriched because we live with and breathe in the ghosts of the past in our homes through the everyday things that were used and held dear in the home of my husband's beginnings.

એ

Breathe in Your Family History
As you walk through your home think about the furniture and possessions you take for granted every day. *What memories and connections do they hold in the light of your family history?* How can you treasure them and pass them down to your loved ones?

MEADOW WALK

Crickets saw their songs in a chorus
of harmony with the full-throated frogs
as the tall grass swishes
    my ankles with soft stroking.
My walk through the meadow
    in the clear light of full, sunned summer
is a bounty of sensual stimulation.
Color arrests my eyes, blinding
    me in smears of yellow and white clumps of daisy,
hot orange daylily, pink purple thistle nodding
      in approval as I wander.
Sharp scents fill my pores as I take in
    the spicy sweet fragrances erupting from each footfall.
Buzzing bees and the jetlike whirling sound
      of humming birds
    assail my ears, soothed and smoothed out by the
    call of a meadowlark or a chickadee.
As a hawk swoops down to capture its mouse or mole prey,
    I enter deeper and deeper
      to the mystery of the meadow.
I am a foreigner here in the harmony of this
    self-sufficient ecosystem.
Will my crunching step set off the balance of nature's
    remarkable order? The pollen caught deftly in my
      shoe will change next year's flower stand;

mice scuttle in frightened flurrying to another
    secret hidden place in the grass;
ants are crushed and birds cry out their warning chirps.
But somehow the meadow will go on and on until the
    next bulldozer arrives to raze her fertile breasts.

§◊§

Drink in the Beauty of Nature
Over the next few days focus on ways to become
one with nature. Drink in her beauty and enter
deeply into her ordered grace. *What order in nature
is destroyed in the name of progress in your neighborhood? What can you do to keep the earth green?*

FOOTPRINTS

In my wanderings from
place to place, I encounter
the uniqueness of human enfleshment.
Stories of happy marriages,
saddened by the deep loss of a spouse;
stories of terrible couplings held together
by steel bands of violence
whirl in and about my mind.
Lives lived in compassionate care for a sick parent,
a mentally challenged child,
or a wheelchair-bound partner
lift my heart to generous self-gift.
Hearts shattered by broken bitterness
or joyous with the lilt of new love
quicken my pulse to penetrating tenderness.
Of all the places I journey,
of all the people who pour out their lives
on the platter of confidence and companionship,
I am enriched and energized.
They trusted enough to walk through my heart
and forever I am marked by their footprints.

Who Has Walked through Your Heart?
Think about the people you have met over time and
some of the conversations you might have had. *What
is the shape and size of the footprints they left on your
heart?* Take these memories and treasure them, seeking to discover the strands that connect you to others.
A web of delicate threads binds us, one to the other.

CLARITY ON A SUMMER'S DAY

There is a boldness in the
straight stand of pink and purple tiger lilies,
a glint that dances off the wind chimes,
    a sultry smoothness hovering in the air,
a juicy ripeness in the taut skin of the tomatoes.
Summer brings a clarity to everything
    as my eye hovers the outdoor space.
Inside I savor the warm sun on the skin of my soul,
    bright-winged musings flutter in
        and through my thoughts,
energy saps up my body and imagination blooms
        in colored profusion,
    my spirit soars on calm, cloudless breeze
        as the air currents sail me away.
There is an inner clarity to summer's day
        that is free for the taking.
    It's just like breathing. Perhaps it's praying!

&❀&

Savor a Summer's Day
Nature connects us to our self and ultimately to
God. *What does a summer's day connect within you?*
Beyond you?

NOSTALGIA

Over cherry Cokes
    at the soda fountain counter
       we spent our breaks.
I, a cashier
      he, a frozen food packer.
That dime store our meeting place—a time
    to convey a certain look, to brush fingertips
        across a waist
        in an electrically charged second.
The ten-minute break, never long enough
    to say all we wanted, to be coy enough or witty.
"Young Love" was the song that
    year I met the boy
    some day to be the man I married.
A few years ago, cherry Cokes
    returned, packaged in cans, nothing
       like the fountain ones with real cherry syrup.
The dime store has been replaced
    with megastores with coffee shops instead of
       soda fountains.
But the spark of those first "young love" years
    returns with a certain look, a brush of the fingertips.

⁂

Remember the First Time
Remember back to the first time that you experienced
the connection of intimacy, shared with another. *What
stands out in your emotional memory? How has that
experienced formed and shaped you even today?*

THE BUTTERFLY KISS

When she was only two or three, my granddaughter gave me a great gift. It was a butterfly kiss. Her mother taught her this tender and endearing act of love. A butterfly kiss is one where you flutter your eyelash on the cheek of another. When Elizabeth spent the night she would always say goodnight with a butterfly kiss and often she would crawl into my bed in the morning lavishing me with eyelash flutters. It became our "thing."

As I struggle to forgive her father for the abuse he inflicted upon my daughter, I need only remember the butterfly kiss. While we may never be reconciled, for that takes mutual desire, I can make the twisting, laborious journey to forgive. Without him I would never know the pure delight of a butterfly kiss. I can only offer the gift of forgiveness in return for her gift of a flutter on the cheek.

Journey toward Wholeness
When you discover and name the gift of love, even from a painful source, you are on the journey of wholeness. *What disconnections have revealed love in your life? How can you offer this gift to another?*

ANIMATED BY THE SAME SPIRIT

We've looked at the moon, wondered at her pocked face and waning, waxing cresting. We've wished upon a star and been awed at shooting tails of shimmering shine. But when we beheld the earth for the first time from the famous space photo, we fell in love with ourselves. We were filled with wonder in seeing the whole extended earth-body as one. This living, pulsing body—earth—alive with souls in many shapes and sizes, backgrounds and cultures *is connected.* All earth's life forms breathe as one; all are part of the same spirit.

To love ourselves we must naturally evolve into falling in love with everything, everyone. Compassion with self will overflow into care for all. The insulated world of a solitary life is impossible once we catch a glimpse of the implications of this deep union. We are small, yet we play a vital role in the whole piece. Energy, the life of the soul, exudes throughout each part of the whole—flowing, sparking newness. With this daunting realization it becomes vitally necessary that we care for each person, each region of the planet, each of the possible planets, galaxies and universes, for all are connected. How can we discard and disregard anything of the whole without discarding and disregarding our very selves? The earth cries out to us to transform our way of being, living, consuming, wasting. It is not enough to reuse, restore and recycle; we must change our soul—our attitudes and behaviors. We must tune our spirit to the spirit of the earth and rediscover who we truly are.

※

Tune in to the Spirit of the Planet
Find a photo of the earth from outer space. Allow it to enter your spirit. *How does the soul of the planet cry out to you to love, to care, and to change?*

CLAIMING THE CONNECTIONS

Try this ritual to celebrate the connections in your life.

To Prepare

Gather photographs, mementos given to you by significant others and some articles from the seashore, a mountain vacation, or your own backyard. Find a place that is quiet, where you will not be interrupted for a time. Light a candle; scatter flower petals and play music that reminds you of summer. Look through the photos as you play the music, allowing your body to relax and your spirit to become still.

The Ritual

Continue to quiet your whole being as you invite the Creator of all life to be present in your ritual time. When you are ready, select any item that seems to beckon, whether a photo, a gift of nature, or a memento. Gently hold the item in the palms of your hands and remember the connections it holds with your past and with past relationships. Continue to hold the item, bringing it close to your heart. Listen, now, to the stories of connection it tells you. Finally, when you are ready, lift the item as high as you can and give thanks for the oneness you experience. Continue reverencing the other objects that evoke a sense of union for you in the same way: holding, embracing and lifting. When you feel you have finished, you may choose to journal your experience. You can celebrate this ritual several times throughout the summer season of your soul.

Autumn

INTRODUCTION

Autumn is a time of reaping. In its brilliance, this fall season of the soul evokes a rich harvest of gifts, gratitude and generosity. But we cannot reap autumn's harvest without watchful rest. The spirit needs the sustenance of autumn's abundance to nurture and prepare itself to meet the solitary surrender of winter's call.

Discovering the gift of each day and responding with a grateful heart and a generous spirit are the heart and soul of this season. But we are lured on by the desire for more—there is never enough money, time, success, recognition, possessions, or affirmation. The problem is that we fail to look at life from the inside out. Instead we are frazzled by running after those things outside ourselves and find that we are tired and unhappy. Essentially, to actualize the power of autumn's abundance, we must turn around our way of looking at life. We must begin with the soul, discover the gifts that make us unique. Each person is gifted; everyone has something distinctive and extraordinary to offer to the universe. Without these particular gifts the whole cosmos will be lacking an important piece on our mutual journey to wholeness. It takes stillness and silence with one's self to discover these graced (freely given) gifts. Autumn is a season that invites us to name, claim, and develop our unique giftedness.

The movement outward continues by taking time to express gratitude for the gifts that make each of us who we are. This is expressed each time we acknowledge a compliment, each time we use our gifts, and each time we offer thanks to the Giver of All Gifts. Finally, the plentitude of this season reminds us to nurture a generous heart in freely giving our gifts back to the universe. Wherever there is a need, there is someone to fill the void. Generous giving marks this season to refresh our soul. Genuine gratitude makes for a happy and fulfilled spirit.

APPLESAUCE

Rich red apples hang from the orchard trees,
low enough for the children to pick and pop
   into large paper sacks.
Every fall we drove to the orchard for the picking time.
Happy autumn day of harvesting
rewarded in the teeth-crunching first bite,
      reveling in that juicy, creamy white flesh,
   sugar-ripe juice dripping off the lower lips.

Apple pies, cobblers baked up as the
   family cored and peeled and prattled away.
Hot cinnamon smells emerging as our
      mouths watered for the first warm taste.

But my favorite time is making the applesauce.
No peeling or coring, just quartering and popping
   into a kettle to simmer all afternoon.

As the cooling light dips lower, alone in the quiet house,
I stir and strain the puddle of thick,
   fleshy apples, softened to mush.
Poured into glass jars the sauce is frozen
   for those winter meals when the sweet smells
      of crunchy harvest seem a dim memory.
Savored times alone with apples poaching are just
   the solitary silence I need to comfort my soul
      and center my spirit.

Treasured Memories
Remember times spent alone in the midst of autumn's
bounty. *What memories do you treasure? What
lessons do this season's bounteousness teach you?*

OF GOLDENROD
AND OTHER SUCH SENTIMENTS

There is a certain nostalgia that hits early every fall. Just as the chrysanthemums come into bloom, there is a plant that sweeps over drainage ditches, roadsides, and vacant parcels of land that vies for my attention. It is the goldenrod, notorious for the allergic sneezing and wheezing she brings about. But that is not my reason for being charmed by this bright flaxen plant. Goldenrod reminds me of the fresh feeling borne by that back-to-school time and all the potential it holds.

Yes, goldenrod graced the cover of those tablets of yellow, lined newsprint that were handed out each year in my grade school. Goldenrod was not just a label; an actual picture of the flower decorated the front cover and, after all, the paper inside was golden. This time of getting ready for school, just as the summer vacation got boring, carried with it a sense of something new and something more. So much for grammar-school musings.

Goldenrod reminds me that fall is a time of possibilities. As I prepared my own children for the new school year I remembered the goldenrod, with a longing for that same sense of fresh starts. Even when I taught school, I prepared lesson plans with an optimism filled with hope for the new students I would touch and the inherent potential of all we would learn together. While goldenrod bears a rash of allergies for some, to me it is also a gift, signaling a season of fresh new possibilities.

Look Again

There are many sides, plusses, and minuses
to everything. As you think of things that seem
to cause a negative response in you, look again,
this time more closely, to find out what potential
for goodness they also bear.

SO MANY GIFTS

I meet them in the quilting classes I teach and even on the quilting retreats—women who feel inadequate, with little sense of accomplishment. It usually begins with a self-disclaimer; "I really can't sew!" "I make a mess out of every project I begin!" "I have no sense of color and design!" By the end of our time together, however, I hope to have given them a sense of their inner gifts, mined through the rudimentary skills involved in making a quilt.

Jacquie is a very large woman who can barely carry in her machine. At each stage of the quilting process, she worries about "getting it right." Yet in her I discover a wonderfully creative spirit. Her delicate fabrics blend into a wash of pastels that remind me of an impressionistic painting. As she frets about the accuracy of her stitches, I keep reassuring her that a quilt is very forgiving, hiding all sorts of off-track stitching in the wrinkled folds of fabric. By the end of our time together, the perfection of sewing fades away, as Jacquie discovers the freedom of enhancing her quilt with intricate rows of decorative stitching.

As Angie begins quilting, she explains that her quilt will be an interpretation of various scenes from her family's history. She uses photographs transferred onto cloth, flower designs that grow in her garden, and a variety of stars. As she works on her quilt her story tumbles out. Her quilt is an attempt to reconnect with her family of origins. She is the only surviving family member after a tragic car accident. This quilt becomes a way of sharing her grief. While Angie has suffered much loss, her grief becomes her gift to the others at the quilt retreat. Her story rolls back the stone sealing the tombs we all use to set aside the emotional toil of our losses in order to "keep on keeping on."

Lynette seems very quiet at first. Her quilt is a patchwork of many fabrics, no one piece the same. She concentrates on cutting and sewing the nine-patch blocks and patiently rips stitches on seams that are crooked. Her fingers bent and misshapen by arthritis can barely hold a needle, but Lynette perseveres. After several sessions together, she finally begins to talk. Her beautiful patchwork of many pieces is being made for children who lost a parent. The cloth comes from the favorite garments of the dead mom or dad. Lynette makes quilts for these children so they can wrap themselves in their lost parent's clothing and imagine they are being hugged. She began to share the gift of a "hug from heaven" after she lost her spouse and made quilts for her own small children.

Everyday gifts often go unnoticed and are disregarded as "no big thing." But each of us is a surprise bag filled with immeasurable delights that lie dormant until someone notices.

୧୦୨

Open the Gift Box of Your Spirit
The most ordinary task is laden with your unique giftedness. As you go through the day notice the talents needed to do what you do naturally. Think of ways to share these with others. *What treasure lies deep within the gift box of your spirit?*

INSIDE THE CLOUDS

Gray, slate clouds
scuttle across leaded sky,
as the bite of chilled, crisp winds
    bite into my bared face.
Autumn's ambiance accompanies me
    on that long walk in moldy-leafed, drizzled drab decay.
On the road, again, a journey, I muse:
    What pilgrim does not wonder at the relevance
        of all this forward thrusting into the unknown?
    What traveler into the trysts of intimacy
        with the Creator
        does not seek meaning out of life's pain?
These dismal days my journey is heavy
        with dark clouds of not knowing,
    not feeling, not connecting,
        so great is my restlessness, fear and fatigue.
When I think to embrace, to enfold myself
    in the desolate dark mantle
        of those dismaying discontentments,
    I find the truth of my perplexing reality!

There is an incomprehensible magnificence in the image
        into which I have been molded—formed,
    shaped by the trials of one lived pilgrimage into the
Unknowing Cloud of Meaning.
        Grace-full and grace-filled I walk on,
    one step at a time gathering the treasures
        of time-aware travel, leaning in on me
            in this ashen-clothed autumn season.

You Have Suffered

When you look back at the suffering in your life,
do you ever wonder how you survived? Not only
that, you learned great truths from your experiences
of pain and doubt. *What gifts were hidden in the gray
clouds of life's travails? What have you gleaned from
the difficulties encountered on your journey? How
have you been brought closer to the Creator of all in
these experiences?*

GIFTS FROM THE EARTH

When I was very young I had no problem trying different foods. Perhaps it was because I got a lot of attention from the adults in my extended family when I had my first taste of pickled herring or jellied pigs feet. But the most wonderful taste treat of an unusual nature happened every fall. Fall was the season when the pomegranate could be found in the grocery store. While my parents were on a tight budget, they splurged every now and then for this exotic and expensive treat. For me, fall meant the possibility of biting into the red juices of pomegranate seeds.

You would never expect that under that rusty-red leather skin lie the fruit's most unusual interior. It seemed that each fruit held a thousand little juicy seeds each section protected by an opaque paper-like membrane. You had to work at getting a mouthful of seeds, but the tart tang of the delicate fruit burst in your mouth with every bite. Tasting somewhat like a cranberry or a juicy apple, the pomegranate was fascinating to examine. I never could figure out the pattern of its sections. Very different from the regular sections of an orange or grapefruit, the seeds coil around in their own intricate maze.

This childhood gift of the pomegranate holds a mystery that never ceases to amaze me. It reminds me that in the most unusual places or under the strangest outer cover lies the possibility of something delicate, delicious and extraordinary. Isn't it that way with people too?

Recall Your Special Gifts

Remember some of the gifts of the earth that have held a surprise for you. Recall some of the people you have found to be far more delightful than you first imagined. *What gifts have you discovered in the most unusual places and under the oddest outer appearances?*

FULL OF GRACE

Grace is that elusive something that opens wide the possibility of something more, something bigger and beyond our little lives. Some would describe it as the Divine chasing us, even when we prefer to run away. Others see grace as a free-flowing fountain of gift that discloses the goodness of the human heart. Whether a matter of fate or faith, grace is a very real and uncanny occurrence in the human experience.

One cannot earn grace or store it up in a hoarding fashion. It flits in and out of life's growing pains with an amazing persistence. Think about the addict who tries to remain sober after many different kinds of treatment, and then one day it works. Grace prevails and some small detail of life triggers a transformation of behaviors, values and attitudes.

Grace usually doesn't hit us over the head in magnificent moments of falling off a horse or God's voice in a burning bush. The normal appearance of grace can be found instead in the small, ordinary events of a life, when we aren't even looking for the gift. Who hasn't heard stories of someone finding a way out of depression because of a smile from a store clerk or being inspired to help the poor by a chance encounter with a homeless beggar?

Grace pervades the very fiber of the created universe. We are told this in the stories surrounding the creation events. After each day of creating the universe and all its bounty of gifts, the Creator saw that *everything was good*. While it may be difficult to see the innate goodness in a tornado that destroys, a ravaging, wild animal that kills a child, a poisonous plant that causes severe illness, or a murderous heart that has no reverence for life; grace does find its way into the nooks and crannies of all that exists. To unearth the gift of grace in each moment of existence and each particle of the created world is the vital responsibility of humankind. With our imagination, our free will, our capacity to feel and determine our course in life, human beings are equipped to rediscover the basic goodness that threads its way throughout this wild and wonderful world and every creature in it. This very way of perceiving and discovering is of itself grace.

⚜

Unearth the Gift of Grace
Think about the way grace pops into your life
and forever changes you by some chance event.
From these recollections, make a list of the gifts
of goodness you have unearthed in your lifetime.
Write down your ideas about grace.

WOMAN OF GRACE

Years ago, I came across the translated journal of a little-known holocaust victim, Etty Hillesum. The spiritual journey of this young woman of Holland has threaded its way through my life like a fine weaving over these many years. An intelligent young woman with degrees in law, Slavonic languages and psychology, Etty began her diary in Amsterdam in July of 1942, about the same time Anne Frank, hidden in a house a few miles away, began her writing. Her journal entries express the core of her search for the essential human dimensions of life in spite of the inhumanity surrounding her. Throughout the process she develops an enormous spiritual conviction that takes her through imprisonment and eventually death at Auschwitz. Some gems that have kept me on the path to truth on my journey are taken from her journal, *An Interrupted Life* (Henry Holt, 1996).

She offers this description of how the inner Spirit speaks to us and grasps our attention: *"Some mornings I wake up with a complete sentence in my head, a few words I must have said to myself softly in the middle of the night, half asleep . . . after I had lain awake for a bit, this phrase from out of the night came to me:* 'A gradual change from the physical to the spiritual.' "

Later, Etty moves deeper into uncovering the mysteries of the spiritual realm and helps us understand that which is larger than life. *"I stood on the little bridge and looked across the water; I melted into the landscape and offered all my tenderness up to the sky and the stars and the water and to the little bridge. And that was the best moment of the day."*

The reality of life is not smothered in lovely ideas. She faces the harsh truth of human dysfunction in spite of the Divine as she moves through her spiritual journey. *"It is sometimes hard to take in and comprehend, oh God, what those created in Your likeness do to each other in these disjointed days. But I no longer shut myself away in my room, God, I try to look things straight in the face, even the worst crimes, and to discover the small, naked human being amidst the monstrous wreckage caused by man's senseless deeds. I don't sit here in my peaceful flower-filled room, praising You through Your poets and thinkers. That would be too simple . . ."*

As her belief in God continues to intensify, Etty finds the spiritual way into the heart of suffering in peace. *"But one thing is becoming increasingly clear to me: that You cannot help us, that we must help You to help ourselves. And that is all we can manage these days and also all that really matters; that we safeguard that little piece of You, God, in ourselves . . . no one is in their clutches who is in Your arms. I am beginning to feel a little more peaceful, God, thanks for this conversation with You."*

⚜

Find That Little Piece of You
Try reading a copy of Etty Hillesum's diary. Take time to reflect upon her words to look at the truth of your own journey. You may be inspired to begin your own spiritual journal.

COLOR ME . . .

What color would you call
      the dancing delights of autumn?
Would it be the golden time,
      light flashing on saffron leaves that wave
   their arms high in adulation?
Or perhaps the creamy orange
      of pumpkin nestled comfortably
         in easy chairs of green, goarded mounds?
How would you paint the colors of fall's flights of fancy
      that blow through your every pore
         in the chilled light that comes so early?
Would scarlet be adequate on her round, waxy apples,
      or russet, rustling leaves of sugar maple
         to capture the undiminished beauty of this season?
Maybe brown, not the plain brown of dirt,
      but the reddish brown of bark, glistening
         in the light after the cold rain illuminates
            the landscape.
Under the steel-blue fall sky, all is a rainbow
      of color, a palate of deep, rich hues—warm, friendly
      colors that gift the earth in brilliance and blaze forth
         to illuminate the very soul of creation.

What Color Is Fall?
Try capturing the warmth of autumn's colors
by painting or making a collage. Just find colors
that are "fall" to you and put them together. *How
does the warmth of these hues touch your spirit
in spite of the cooling weather?*

THE AUTUMN OF LIFE

It happens sometimes after midlife;
  that brilliant, shining time
    when the glint of wisdom seeps
    through the prism of our souls.
It's the russet richness of past perception
    gleaned from experience—a sharpened
      nib that paints our lives
with acknowledgment, appreciation and awareness
for the simpler pleasures
      and hidden sagacity to be discovered under rocks
        of prejudice, partiality and naivete,
          blocking the sunlight
    bounced off golden boughs.
It's the golden hope of future fecundity for generations
    that pour from the loins of crimson thighs on old oaks,
      promise of what can be—possibility.
Knowing all will be well in spite
    of twisted, tortuous paths that seem to lead nowhere.
Autumn is the season of a life well lived, beyond the risk
    of obliteration, lived in ever widening circles
        that pool with love's
      gleaming glory, lived in the rapture that delights
in the everyday—every day.

蒓

In Sync with the Season
What is the season of your life right now? This
question does not imply a chronological season,
for the timelessness of the spirit is a *kairos* affair.
How would you describe your "autumn" season?

IT IS ALL OVER

When she was in her early eighties, she thought her life was over. Still bowled over by the death of her husband, with whom she had a relationship for over fifty years, the woman grieved and made stutter starts at going on without his companionship. All seemed like a dream. She wandered through life in the fog of bereavement. It was like swimming in a sea of thick syrup; no energy to survive, not knowing or caring if the next day would ever come.

We talked over and over again about the depressing state that shrouds this time of mourning. I felt helpless to lift her out of this listless state. I read to her from my journal and gave her poems to etch the memory of the beloved and spread out a blanket of gifts he left as legacy to all the family.

She reluctantly took a small step toward reconstructing her life when I gave her a blank book to journal her memories. With a faltering pen she started to record what she did every day. Soon she was able to write down her feelings of loss and grief. Eventually, a torrent of words fell from the pen in her trembling hand as she expressed her inner thoughts; conversing with her spouse in love letters and shared memories. Expressions of gratitude for the small things of life—waking up in the morning, being alive—were scribed onto the pages. A lasting testament to her life, this journal became a fount of healing and energy, a source of life for one who thought it was all over.

Journal to Discovery

Try working through your life experiences with the
help of a journal. If you have never journaled, begin
by noting the events of your day at a specific time
each day. If you already journal, try a new format—
gratitude lists, letters to yourself, conversations
with God or poetry. Look back on past journals
to discover where you were in the spiritual quest,
to discover how much you have grown.

SURPRISINGLY, NOT WHAT YOU THINK

When I spotted her in the airport, I immediately thought "another case of the oppression wrought on women." She was clothed in a dark-colored, long dress and covered with a scarf, so that no part of her hair escaped its folds. Large, dark, almond-shaped eyes appeared weary with the prospect of travel accompanied by her brood. She was making the long flight to Israel with her husband, dressed in Western attire, and her six children. I quickly averted my eyes, trying not to stare in pity . . . or was I judging her husband, freed from the traditional Muslim garb?

As I approached my seat, I recoiled—no sleep for me on the eleven-hour night flight, for in the seat next to mine was the woman and her youngest, a six-month-old baby boy. Not wanting to appear rude or to cross the lines of respect due another culture, I tried to mind my own business. But to no avail; the grandmother in me couldn't restrain a helping hand when she tried to find a bottle of milk to calm her crying child. So I held him for her as she rifled through several bags. This began a long night of conversation and the realization of my prejudices and own need to judge, to categorize.

She was returning to her hometown of Nazareth—like another exiled mother—with her five sons, a teenage daughter, and her husband. While she reveled in the freedom of movement in the United States, she feared the violence meted upon her family because they were different. Her husband's two brothers were both murdered for drug money as they tended the family grocery store. She longed to raise her children in a place where they would not run the risk of being orphaned.

As the night wore on, I learned that her way of dress was a choice that she had made only a few years ago. It was not oppressive but a spiritual sign of her commitment. I watched as the Arab father gently guided his very well-behaved boys in their choice of age-appropriate movies and video games. I saw the beauty of family life and committed love that was different than my experience, but so very much the same. I discovered how much more I needed to weed out the narrow-mindedness that grows in the cracks of my spirit, like so many weeds among the wheat. I discovered the gift of a modern Madonna in that long night flight that will forever remind me of the many paths to communion.

❦

Me, Prejudiced?
Recall times when you were confronted with your own prejudices and need to compartmentalize others who are different. *What gifts lie under the surface of these encounters?*

ASSESSING PERSONAL GIFTS

Find time this week to go to a quiet place where you will not be disturbed. In that place surround yourself with things that ease your spirit—lighted candles, incense, flowers, cushions, and/or soothing music. When you are ready, calm your inner voice by concentrating on your breathing and your heartbeat. Sink into your deepest self, the place where your spirit resides and encounters the Spirit of Life.

Imagine that you find yourself in a lush wood aglow with the brilliance of autumn. You listen as the squirrels scurry about on crunching leaves. Geese fly in formation overhead, honking their fall, farewell flight. You wander down a path, pulled by some unknown source until you arrive at a clearing. There, in the middle of this leafy grotto, sits a person you recognize immediately. This is a person you know to be wise, a mentor of sorts, someone you trust. The wise one beckons you to come and sit in the clearing and you move forward in confidence and comfort. *Who is your wise one? What do you feel as you join him or her?*

Enjoined in a conversation, you find yourself confiding in the wise person, speaking of your past experiences. You recall several times when you were "put-down" or disregarded as you offered your opinions or services to others. *What do you remember of these negative experiences?* The wise one helps you remember the other times when you changed the course of things by speaking out or acting. *What comes to mind as a positive accomplishment?* As you converse, you become aware of the many gifts and talents you have honed over the years. *Enumerate some of these in your inner conversation.*

The wise one speaks to you of the potential gifts that remain for you to develop. *What might these gifts be?*

As you prepare to leave this place of encounter with wisdom, know that you can return any time. Allow your spirit to rise to the surface and return to the room—the reality of now.

※

Let Your Spirit Rise
Take your journal or a blank sheet of paper and make a list of the gifts which you have already used to change the lives of others. On a second page write down those gifts that germinate in your deepest self. *Name some ways in which you can claim and grow these gifts.* Remember, the world is transformed by the smallest offerings of a sincere spirit.

MOONWALK

Harvest moon
round orange
   pumpkin in the sky
the circle without end or beginning.
All connected, never ending
   spiraling down . . .
     down into the recesses—the source—
      the still-point
Where ALL has being.
So joined to the moon, this fragile life
   sparks into orange glow,
   gifting the universe in simple ways.
The tenderest touch on old wrinkled hands, gnarled
   and bent out of shape—care carries on!
The look of love passes quickly between lovers
   across the breach of a crowded chasm, speaking,
     "You belong!"
The listening ear, tuned to grieving hearts
     and confused souls,
   takes time so well spent in assuring affirmations!
The care of a flower,
gentleness with a child,
   stroking of a pet,
     pleasuring in birdsong,
all simple gifts
that make the moonglow in bright brilliance
   sublime radiance on a dark fall night.

Glowing in the Moonlight
Take a walk on a night when the harvest moon
is full. As you look at the moon, think about
your connection to this reflective, glowing sphere.
What simple gifts can you offer the moon to intensify
her light?

EROSION TO EXPANSION

There is nothing like the workplace to erode one's confidence and spirit. Far too often the hard work and diligence of women and men is overlooked in lieu of profit and efficiency. The extension of work to ten and twelve-hour days is becoming the norm. The older worker who attempts to use her or his gifts for the betterment of the whole is often erased as "stuck in old patterns." Even the younger employee's ideas are passed over when he or she is not willing to devote every waking hour to the firm and its mission to make more money faster and more efficiently. Women find themselves in the dilemma of climbing up the ladder of success in a corporate milieu where everything is still geared to the executive who has a spouse at home to take care of the "other" things in life. Men, too, discover that the college degree is not a ticket to security in the workplace, nor are their gifts appreciated if they diverge from the corporate image of "one of the boys." Success is measured in stock values, profit and the bottom line, rather than on what the company and product are contributing to the common good.

In this environment, it is more important than ever to maintain a sense of confidence, continually developing the potential gifts within. This concern is about the dignity of the human person and the common good, two values eroded and undermined in the workplace. Therefore, it is vital that we balance out the negative impact of being erased and ignored, with some positive exercises to continually name and grow one's gifts.

The first step is to be *honest* about the gifts one does have. The source of some of this lack of confidence in one's giftedness is to think everyone else has all the gifts or to want the gifts of others, blocking out the ability to see one's own talents. To determine the giftedness that lies within, take time to reflect upon what has been accomplished and the talents needed to achieve that success. Time alone, looking back, and honest evaluation are some of the ways to name and claim one's contribution to the common good.

Furthermore, good friends are honest in their appraisal of one's talents. *Notice* your reaction when affirmed or complimented. Disclaimers often get in the way of growing our gifts. Especially when used in the workplace, disclaimers such as, "Oh, that was nothing!" slough off the image of a self-assured person. The input of good friends, relatives, and mentors are especially helpful in honing and fortifying one's sense of giftedness. *Thank* these people when a compliment is offered; *invite their input* to discern additional gifts.

Finally, it is important to realize that our gifts are constantly changing, old talents diminish, and new ones come to the fore. *Pay close attention* to the energy drain and energy release in your day-to-day activities. When your energy is heightened it can be a sign of a new talent emerging. New challenges are important environments in developing and honing new gifts. *Risk* trying new things to discover transformative growth within.

⚜

Pay Attention

Notice how you handle affirmation. When complimented, remember the talents it took to earn that affirmation. Try something new to unearth potential gifts. *What energy, what transformation builds up in you as you attempt a new challenge?*

SELF-ASSURANCE

The young single mother spent her days in a demanding job. As a teacher, she found herself bogged down in the extracurricular activities and political dimensions of her job. She loved the classroom and even the preparation and follow-up with her students. But the time spent in meetings, endless paperwork, and showing up at politically important events after hours demanded that she spend less time with her child. With the help of mentors and friends who reassured her of her talent for writing and her ability to clearly articulate complicated scientific information, she took a risk. Now a freelance science writer, she spends her time at home and more easily manages quality time with her daughter. She can adjust her schedule to be present at important events in her child's life. While she took a large cut in pay and runs the risk of uneven income, this single parent discovered a new way of life that has built her self-esteem and integrated her values.

Another woman, who felt she had no marketable skills, found she had to join the workforce after her children moved out of the house and her husband died. With honest introspection and the affirmation of friends and family, she decided to follow her passion—knitting. Now manager of a small specialty company, she designs patterns for knitters around the world. Through the Internet and personal instruction she teaches knitting and designs unique sweaters for small boutiques. Self-confident, this woman now emanates the joy present when energy and passion sustain one's life work.

Now over eighty years old, this woman of wisdom continues to work. She became a beautician at the early age of sixteen, during the depression. This work not only gave her an opportunity to contribute to the family expenses, but also gave her a sense of worth. She worked part-time while raising her family. During this time in her life the work put her in touch with wealthy women who had troubles and crises. Her ability to listen gave them a sense of worth and reminded her that her own problems were not unique. Later in life she continued to make women feel beautiful inside and out. It energizes her spirit to give others a "little boost." She continues to beautify and listen today—not because of the income, but as a social outlet and a way to use her gifts to help others feel self-confident. The energy that comes from using one's gifts to reach out to others can keep one young in body and spirit in spite of chronological age.

⚜

What Keeps You Centered?

Think about people that you know who seem to love what they do. Look at their lives and the model of giftedness they present to the world. The secret lies in not emulating their lives and wishing for their gifts, but in discovering your own talents and passion. *What focuses your life and keeps you centered? How do your passion, your talent, and your circumstances combine to lead you to transform your life's work in order that you might live out of your self-assurance?*

BANQUET OF LIFE

Poured out upon the cloth of mossy green,
a garden cornucopia of fresh harvest;
squashes in green, pale yellow-peach,
orange and yellow-white,
apples of every imagined flavor, colored
in reds and greens,
bright green beans, purple smooth-skinned
eggplant,
crisp pointed fingers of orange carrot
and creamy white parsnip
tumble in an array of jewel tones,
delighting your savory soul.
The generous bounty of the Mother:
from her deep, dark earth womb
spill forth a harvest to
delight the eye and feed the body and soul.
What thanks can we offer for such a feast?
What libation is Earth Mother's due?
First fruits in days of old
offered in solemn ritual.
But today, crumbled earth tracks are washed away,
fruits of the earth in sterile plastic
line shelves of stores—
not cascading down mossy banks.
No offering to the source—
the plentitude of Mother's womb—
Some know not this cradle of harvest birth.

How can we just take and eat without a blessing—
a fleeting thought of thanks?
No, it is time to acknowledge earth's generous bounty
with our own generous spirit.
Without ties or strings attached
we join in a chorus of genuine generosity,
sharing the meal, breaking the bread,
and remembering
the unconditional generosity
of the Earth Mother.

❦

We Give Thanks for Your Bounty
As you shop for groceries this week, think about the
origins of the produce, the source of the foods that
sustain life. In your own way, try to imitate the
generosity of Earth Mother by sharing a meal and
your time with others. *What are some other ways you
can give thanks for earth's plentitude?*

GENEROUS SOULS

I t is refreshing to meet generous, self-giving persons in this culture of bustling about. They are models for the world of the adage, "it is far more important to give than receive." Grandmothers who give up careers to care for grandchildren when parents have to work or are unfit abound in our society. That neighbor down the street who shares her garden's bounty with everyone, keeping all supplied with fresh tomatoes and zucchini. The widow who volunteers her time teaching adults how to read, opening the doors to a new pleasure and discovery for others.

I have had the opportunity to observe generosity, beyond the boundaries of the ordinary. I was traveling with my parents when we were rerouted to another city because of a sudden blizzard in our hometown. Grounded for two days and nights, I helped them cope with finding a place to stay and tracking the flight cancellations until we were safely outbound to our destination.

But the real act of generosity occurred when we boarded the original flight. It was then that I noticed a mentally challenged adult escorted onto the plane by a stewardess. She had a note pinned on to her blouse, with instructions for the airline personnel who would meet her when we landed. When news of our change of plans was announced, I saw that she did not understand. Once on the ground in our rerouted city, the stewardess took her into the long lines waiting to be assigned a hotel room, and left her there. Noticing that she was incapable of finding her way through the dilemma of being stranded, a woman seated near her on the plane took charge. She saw that the note on her blouse had a phone number and she contacted her relatives. This woman went beyond the norm by taking the challenged woman into her hotel room and caring for her the whole time until we were safely bound for our destination. I am not sure that I could give so generously of my self to another, but this woman has remained for me a model of the spirit of self-giving.

⚜

No Strings Attached
Think about the ways in which you have given of yourself without strings attached and about other generous souls. *What examples of self-giving have you observed all around you? How has this affected and motivated your spirit of generosity?*

GIVING THANKS

One way of giving thanks for the wonders of the world and the joy of living is through prayer. But what, exactly, is prayer? It is hard to define, to put your arms around. Rather, some examples might illustrate the ease with which the human spirit prays.

Bill prays in the shower. "I just let the water pour over me and I thank God that I am alive to see another day. I talk about what I will be facing that day and ask for help."

Mary finds time for prayer in the car, while waiting for traffic or to pick up a child from a soccer practice or dance lesson. "Prayer for me is a conversation with the Source—that something that is bigger than life itself. I just quiet myself and remember all the things I am grateful for. Most of the time I ask for help in coping with a problem, guidance on raising my family, or the needs of others who are sick or in trouble. It's like sitting down and having a long talk with a good friend."

Candice tells this story about prayer. "My young daughter must have picked up on the fact that I am in the habit of asking God for a parking space in a crowded mall lot. She told me one day that God must really like me because she noticed that someone would pull out of a spot every time I asked." Isn't that how reliance on a Higher Power begins?

Prayer can be in a quiet space or in a crowded room. It sometimes uses words to thank, to ask, or to express sorrow. There are prayers that are wordless, like looking up at the stars in wonder or marveling at the perfection of a newborn child. Some set aside time for prayer each day or once a week to quiet down and meditate. Others use inspirational books, like the Bible, the Koran, or the Tao Chi to help them reflect upon the spiritual depths of the Unknown. There are many ways of praying, and during the course of our spiritual journey the method of prayer that works best changes. But the human spirit does cry out into the unknown with the faith and hope that Something Greater hears, responds and loves unconditionally.

※

Try a New Way of Praying
Notice when you find yourself praying—even in the simplest way. You may want to try a new way of expressing your thanks to the Source of Love through the ritual prayer on page 133 (Circle of Stones).

BLESSED ARE . . .

Blessed are the children, with no voice,
who teach us to play with carefree abandon,
whose wisdom surpasses that of sages and scholars;
Blessed are the challenged who edify by enduring,
surmounting obstacles incomprehensible to the whole,
handicapped by the blind eye of judgment
and perfection.
Blessed are the homeless for reminding us we must stand
in their place to understand the destructive course
of unchecked consumerism, hoarding,
and having to have it all.
Blessed are the dying who teach us the way
into the unknown and grace us with
sacred memory and unsurpassed courage.
Blessed are the imprisoned who remind us that love
conquers violence, judging us all in the courts
of responsibility for our indifference to
abandonment and abuse in this throwaway society.
Blessed are the least, the underdogs, the marginalized
in our world who cry and claw at our
consciousness to look them in the eye
and know we are "one."

We Are Gifted
The lives torn by the ravages of our culture gift us
with a new wisdom and way of thinking. All people
have a unique gift for us. *What have you learned from
such as these? Who else would you call "blessed"?*

CIRCLE OF STONES

Try this ritual to celebrate the unique giftedness that lies within your spirit.

⟨⟩⟨⟩ To Prepare

On an outdoor walk this week, collect a number of stones that seem interesting to you. Once you have gathered them, clean them off with water and brush off any dirt with a wire brush. When you have a few moments to yourself, take the stones and a permanent marker into a quiet sacred space.

⟨⟩⟨⟩ The Ritual

Sit on the floor and surround yourself with a circle made of the stones. Quiet yourself in a way that is comfortable, allowing your thoughts to run through your recent past. Recall some accomplishments, things you are proud of and activities that renewed your energy. As you think of these events, go deeper and search the depths to determine the gift or talent needed. Print that gift on one of the stones with the marker. Continue in this manner until you have named several gifts and marked your circle of stones. When you feel ready, look around your circle and realize that the gifts that are uniquely "you" radiate out to form the circle. The circle ripples into the world to enrich the human family and indeed all of the created world. Close this ritual by giving thanks for the gifts you possess and by asking for guidance in discovering the gifts that lie in potential within your spirit.

Winter

INTRODUCTION

The winter season is a time of shortened daylight hours, a time of cooling down for the planet, and a time of dormancy for plant and animal alike. This winter season of the soul parallels the path of the sun and planet. Winter's frozen sleep provides an opportunity to let our spirit lie fallow, to rest, and to retrieve. The wild weather of winter can limit our movement, drawing us into the reverie of hibernation. The cold, icy winds lure us deeper into the molten core of our journey inward, warming us to move out again and face the frost-frozen wasteland.

Winter gifts the spirit with wisdom when entered into fully. As we allow this season of the soul to permeate our lives, we discover a well of wisdom within and are united to the source of wisdom—Holy Wisdom. Wisdom is understanding, insight and intuition. Spiritual wisdom goes beyond these defining words. Imagine the dark days of winter and those rare moments when the sun peeks out of the snow clouds to glisten the landscape in blinding light bounced off crystalline snowflakes. Wisdom is this kind of light in the darkness of the soul of the universe. Wisdom is a gathering of all we have learned along the journey of our living, intensifying as we travel. Wisdom penetrates all things, reflecting the eternal light.

This season of the soul explodes into wisdom, inviting us to fully integrate our lives into the cosmos and its source. Winter's beauty and brutality lure us on a path toward facing personal mortality. Winter invites our imagination to run free and our intuition to be a guiding force in order that our spirit might be transformed by the gift of wisdom.

Mortality

In the stark blinding white, punctuated
by the etched limbs of trunked trees,
in this barren, bleached landscape,
   something red flashed through the spiked forest.
A red-tailed hawk rides the icy currents,
   scouring the drifts for its prey.
Caught and killed, the mouse or mole
   became food, energizing the beautiful bird's silent spiral.
Nature gives and takes, feeds and foils!
The bleak, open landscape opens her bosom,
   making effortless the hawk's hunt.
Red tail across the pristine snow,
blood stains on white batting—a killing
      in my yard,
reminders of life's fragility,
   life is but a breath—
      a moment, gone in the blink of an eye.

✵

Reminders of Mortality
Daily reminders of our mortality serve to lead
us into living life to its fullest. *What reminders
of mortality in nature urge you to live today with
your fullest potential?*

FESTIVAL OF FIRE

The longest night and shortest day mark the winter solstice. Have not all of our lives been punctuated with those dark times that never seem to end? Where is the light in the long winter of grief? Will the dawn ever come to the broken feeling of failure in a ruptured relationship? Is there a crack of light that can penetrate the gloom of fear that hangs over hospital waiting rooms? No wonder we fear the dark! Hoping against hope for the dawning light, the ancient ones survived the long darkness of this first winter's day by lighting up hillsides with bonfires and carrying torches in snaking lines toward their sacred places.

What fire then can we light against the fear of darkness in our winter's dreaded days? Wisdom points the way to make it through these dark nights of the spirit. Deep wisdom moves us beyond our selves. It is a pinprick of light for us to follow toward the Source. The wisdom within each human spirit draws us to trust in something more—to surrender to the Unknowable God of Life. The dark of winter is a holy invitation to abandon our fears and lay them at the altar of the universe. In her compassion the Flame of Wisdom will lead us to a new transformation, a new understanding of the place of darkness—a gift that exposes our inner shadows to the light of truth.

※

From Dark to Light
Remember those dark times when your spirit longed for the light of truth. *What new understandings did you discover in the light of the days that followed? How have you been changed through enduring these winter times on your journey?*

JOURNEY INTO THE UNKNOWN

Star of wonder,
    where do you lead?
Path lit by beams,
    blinking, shadowed light.
If I follow—
    who knows where
        or how the journey will go?
Will I find the child—
    beaming light for the world?
The way is fraught with
    tortuous turns;
I lose myself at times
    along its twisting route.
Yet, steady star,
    you twinkle on:
Coaxing, cajoling,
    pulling, pursuing
      me along.

🕉

The Path of the Spirit
The journey of the Spirit is a path into the unknown.
*What pulls you into this path? What twisting and
turning have you experienced along the way?*

FROZEN CLOTHES

Sometimes when I drive through the Amish countryside, I notice that these people dedicated to the simple life hang their wash outside even in the winter. It surely must freeze and then what do they do with them, I wonder. In the warmer months, the overalls and plain dresses billow on the line in every yard. But in winter the clothes just hang there like scarecrows. Most put them on a front porch clothesline to avoid traipsing through snowdrifts in their neatly fenced farmyards.

Curious, I tried it once. Jeans, a few tee shirts and a knit skirt, hung neatly across my deck on a dry wintry day. A neighbor noticing this strange sight called and asked if I wanted to use her electric dryer. I tried to explain my experiment, but she was clearly baffled.

In the waning light of the late afternoon, I went out to retrieve my scarecrows, stiff and straight. It was then that I stopped to watch a bright red cardinal at the feeder. As I took down the clothesline, I heard the crack of the looming trees and in the distance a squirrel family chattered from a nest high up in the frozen branches. Sounds and sights I would have missed if not for my experiment, so closed up tight was my heat-saving home.

Yes, the jeans and shirts were frozen stiff. I had to lay them out over the dryer to thaw. They were damp; probably the dry crackling winter air had removed some moisture from their sodden cloth. The dampness did make pressing the clothes glide with ease. I never found out how the Amish get their clothes dry in the cold winter air, but I did discover the wonder that comes with an excuse to spend time in the cold hanging clothes on a line on my deck.

⚜

Doing Something Different

Think about a time when you tried something that seemed ridiculous or comic. *What lessons about life did you learn?* Use your imagination to prompt you to try something different and see what happens.

LIVING WITH THE DISASTERS

Good comes from living with the disasters that life metes out to every person. This is the beginning of wisdom—discovering the good in the upside-down curve balls thrown at us from time to time.

Meaning and understanding came to Mary as she lived those dying last days with her husband. The meaning of her marriage crystallized in those days of tender care for the beloved of so many years. His dying empowered her with a renewed energy to live a life of giving in what remaining time she had left. Facing death with courage, he eased the discomfort of others with undoubting humor. Mary understood that there is no fear in death, for love has no boundaries. Love endures beyond the grave.

Another family was transformed by the disastrous fire that burned away all their material possessions but could not touch the memories and sense of home found in their togetherness rather than in a structure. The burnt-out shell of a house, frozen still-life scenarios of breakfast dishes, dirty laundry, and a waiting game board were blackened with soot. Yet their light poured forth as they learned to accept the generosity of others and to survive with fewer material possessions. The wisdom of pulling together as a family, the importance of accepting the help of others, and the love they shared was their legacy for a lifetime.

Disaster creeps into the folds of each person's attempts at happiness and comfort. It is the source of unlimited opportunity if one perceives and remains open to the transformative power within each painful experience. Surrounded in the loving embrace of a compassionate God, we grow and heal and discover in the midst of tragedy. This is the stuff of wisdom, that which we seek on this sojourn of the soul.

֍

The Stuff of Transformation

Look back and reflect upon a disastrous event in your life. Remember who you were before the experience and who you became as you worked your way through the suffering. *What transformative changes occurred in you? How have you grown in wisdom?*

WINTER MUSINGS

Winter winds
   rebuff the scattered fragments
     of my soul.
This frigid pre-dawn walk
   to ease the inner conversation
     that crept around the corners of my mind,
   waking me, led me out into the dark.
Faint scuttling sounds
   echo across the frozen space
     magnified by the millions of flakes
       that wash my face awake in an icy bath.
Worry, anxiety, fretting over some dilemma
   woke me as I heed the need for solitude
     to sort and sift the choices arranged
       across the panorama of my frozen imagination.
Seeking release from this unending chatter within
   I am calmed by the wind and wet snow chafing
     frozen skin to a ruddy rigor.
All is quiet now as the slow pink finger of dawn
   leisurely, yet deliberately, appears
     in the eastern sky.
This frozen wasteland and whipping winds ease
   the torrent within, thawing my heart and head,
     propelling me to turn inward
   to melt in the flaming core of my being where
     warmth eases my spirit and stops the clamoring,
   knowing that the clouds dim another sunrise,
     another day, and another possibility.

Where Do You Find Comfort?

Allow the winter cold to move you deeper into the
core of your being. Take whatever makes you
anxious or afraid into that place where you will find
comfort and reassurance. *What do you discover as
you sink deeper into your spirit?*

MAKING CHOICES

Choices fill our days: to wake and go to work or call in sick; what to eat and wear; what to do with this one, wonderful day; and what attitudes will permeate this day. Most choices seem insignificant and are automatic. Yet from time to time we approach a crossroad and have to choose a new and different path. This is risky business for we do not know where we are headed. Choices made out of inner wisdom are actions that contain potential for further growth in this spiritual quest.

Wisdom is the ability to perceive what is being birthed. It is the ability to imagine what is not yet, helping us to straddle the finite and the infinite. Before making an important decision, take time to quietly reflect upon any of these questions that are helpful in discerning the way of wisdom:

What do I seek to create with this one, wonderful life?
Does this choice move me closer to that reality?
What do I hope to cultivate, to set free?
What are the negative and positive consequences of my choices?
What do I hope to gain? What will I lose in making this choice?
How will this choice make me more whole? Will it fragment my being?
What ripple effect will this choice have on others? On the whole of creation?
Does the choice give me energy or does it seem to drain me?
If I imagine myself in this decision, how will I be changed?

*In what direction does the spirit of love, compassion and
generosity seem to lead?*

*Does this choice heal or heighten my fragmented parts—
addictions, fears or past trauma?*

*How does this choice lead me into a deeper union with
God? With myself? With the universe?*

Living the Questions

Use a journal and several times of quiet to reflect
upon these questions. Choose those questions which
seem to fit your situation. Allow these questions to
lead you into deeper, more personal questions as
you seek to make a wise choice.

BIRDS IN THE CHRISTMAS TREE

When we first moved into this home in the woods, we started the tradition of purchasing a balled tree—a Conculor pine—to deck our house for the holidays. This took great planning and physical effort. Late in the fall we would dig a deep hole somewhere in the yard, fill it with leaves, and cover it with a board to prevent accidental twisted ankles.

Usually our sons came home a week before Christmas to help out. Hauling the heavy tree out of the car and onto the porch, where it would remain cool and dormant, was quite a task. On the eve of Christmas we would drag it into the house and decorate it with the memorabilia of accumulated ornaments and lights. But we could only enjoy its glowing presence for a few days. The trauma suffered by the pine if it would come out of dormancy in the warmth of the house would surely kill it. So, faithfully we would undress her boughs and all lend a hand to the perennial planting.

The busyness of our lives, concern for the cutting down of evergreens, and the effects of aging have led us to revel in the resplendent light of an artificial tree. We reasoned that a live tree held its indoor magic for a few fleeting days, while this wire and plastic imitation could be enjoyed for weeks. But I still miss the smells and enchanting marvels of our living tree.

Each season holds a special memory of those strong, solid trees. I observe each spring as birds build their nests in those Christmas trees of old. I am transfixed as I watch the parents flit in and out of the pine boughs to feed their young. I love the smell of pine released as I brush against the needles in my summer gardening. Each waft of fragrant freshness takes

me back to those Christmases past. In the winter, as the
Conculor pines are dressed in white petticoats of snow,
I remember our holy days of celebration and joy when they
spent a few days decking the living room, living with us for
just a while. My imagination sees the trees in the distant yard
waving hello as the wind tosses bough and branch, wishing
us all a merry time.

The Blessings of Change

Our life changes all the time. We resist change, but
it floods in upon our lives in spite of our steadfast
clinging to the way things were. *What changes have
you had to make recently? What blessings can you
discover in the unfamiliar?*

RED COAT IN WINTER

Bounded on all sides by bilious mounds of white snow,
the child in the red coat
    seemed but a dot on the landscape.
But a closer look revealed
  her beckoning gaze,
    a hand raised, ever so slightly,
  that pressed the soul to follow.
"Into the woods, after me," she bid.
A Red Riding Hood on the
  white horizon of the spirit,
    her own path into the unknown forest
      to pull off another kindly deed—
a way out of the maze of violence
  that entraps, engulfs and overwhelms
    the sturdiest of souls . . .
  and so the child shall lead.

❖

The Inner Voice of Wisdom
Reflect upon the wisdom of even the smallest of
children. What is it about life that erodes away this
innate wise spirit? *When have you been led out of
an entrapping situation by following the voice
of wisdom within your soul?*

WISDOM

A labyrinth into undiscovered places—
imagination fueled by a vision of
something more.
Wisdom's ways seek understanding
amidst swirling winds of change—
always trusting in the Source.
She seeks wholeness, integrity, healing,
giving birth to compassion
in her passionate flame of love.
Wisdom invites us to feast
on her finest foods that
fill the spirit—trust, hope, generosity, and joy.
As we walk the maze of life's journey
in the ways of wisdom,
we travel in the company of pilgrims who
haunt this holy path.
Woven together in a holy web of seeking,
our parched souls find fountains
flowing from wisdom's womb;
nourishment to energize
our flagging spirits in her breasts;
the Source and Summit of our holy quest.

❧❀❧

Personify Wisdom
Evoke your imagination to envision the meaning of
wisdom. *How would you personify wisdom? What
images of wisdom tumble out of your musings?*

ESCAPE TO WARMTH

As I sat in the warming sun, a southern escape from the wild winds of winter up north, I struggled with guilt. What right have I to enjoy this peaceful warm place, while my mother lies sick in the hospital? This was nothing life-threatening—but what if something went wrong? Wouldn't a good daughter cancel vacation plans? I deserved some time alone with my husband—that is my first priority. Was I running from responsibility? First children are responsible to an extreme that is not healthy.

In my inner arguing back and forth, the threads of similarity cast a sobering pall on this sunlit day. She was traveling also, when her mother lay dying in a hospital bed. I stood watch at Grandmother's side, telling her stories I remembered from her life. Mother finished her vacation on the sun-kissed shores and Grandmother waited. When she returned, Grandmother drew upon all her strength to revive her ninety-seven-year-old dying body. Mother's guilt spilled over on to me in the waiting room. She cried because she put Grandma into a nursing home and that was how she got this life-threatening flu. She sobbed out her regrets over the years, when she felt she had failed as a daughter. Mom's struggle was so deep, she was afraid to enter the sanctuary of this dying matriarch. I convinced her that even though Grandma was in and out of consciousness she could hear everything. I encouraged her to ask for forgiveness for all these human failings in order to free herself from the guilt. She asked me to accompany her.

The privilege of witnessing this confessional moment of grace was a memory I shall cherish. As Mother spoke her heart and sobbed her deepest sorrow, Grandmother opened her dusty blue eyes, reached for her daughter's hand, and breathed a long sigh as her spirit returned home.

This winter remembering in the warm sun bathed me in an inner light of reassurance that I had chosen well. My spirit reached out to Mom from that distant southern shore and I knew we were closer than ever in this one precious moment.

One Precious Moment

Remember those times when you wrestled with guilt. Think of the ways in which you make choices and be reassured that, guided by an authentic spirit, you have chosen well. *What precious moments of insight and connection have emerged from these inner struggles?*

THE ILLUSION OF CONTROL

So much energy and time are wasted trying to live the illusion of control. Married parents try to control spouses and children to the point of driving them away. At work, employees and employers, sucked in by the need to have power over others, scramble for control to manipulate one another. Addicted to consuming, all are lured into the myth of control by connecting success with more things and newer and bigger material goods. We keep the fires of these addictions alive with great cost to our spirits, our hearts and our inner energy.

The problem is embedded in the illusion itself. We have the mistaken notion that if we can control our surroundings and the people around us, we will be happy, successful and at peace. But control "over," that is, exterior power, is a route that leads nowhere.

To replenish the spirit and recover the soul from within—authentic power—leads us to let go, to surrender to the limits of the day. Daring to defy the cultural lure of the myth of control is a transforming process. Just as the earth yields to the stark dormancy of winter, where all appears dead and dark, we must surrender to the way things are, to the rhythm of living and dying, attaching and detaching, that occurs in every moment of time. Surrender opens our vista to discover our true sense of identity, intimacy and even meaning. Yielding to what is breaks open our passion for life and love, strengthening us to serve the inner vision that illuminates a new path—a new way of being. Letting go is not an option. Love demands that we cultivate the art of releasing one

another. The saying, "The greatest gifts we can give our
children are roots and wings," reminds us of the importance
of letting go. Without surrender, our spirit calcifies into
indifference, bitterness and cynicism. Letting go begins deep
within the core of our souls. From this source the art of
lightly holding and setting love free can flourish into actions.

🕉

Need to Control
Name some of the attachments that bind you into
the illusion of control. As you list these, examine
them to discover the source of your need to control.
*How does power "over" and power from "within" play
out in your daily experiences?*

THE STRENGTH OF SURRENDER

Take time in a quiet place this week to meditate. You may find that quieting music helps you relax. Play it for a time as you sink into the silence of your soul. As the music ends, close your eyes and imagine that you are walking the beach on a bright sunlit afternoon. You carry with you a pail and begin to collect lovely shells and pieces of coral. Each treasure placed into your bucket is carefully selected and carries special delight. As you walk the pail becomes heavy with found treasure. You find that you are hot, sweaty and tired. *What are some of the attachments that you cling to in this moment of time? How does keeping them safe and secure tire or burden you?*

As you continue your walk, wondering why you are expending all this energy, you meet a small child. The child begins to walk with you, matching your large steps with his or her small ones. By this time you are out of breath and your steps slow. The child looks up at you curiously, asking, "Why don't you put down your heavy bucket?" Alarmed, you try to explain that you want to hold on to your treasures. The child offers to carry your load, but you refuse, clinging more tightly to the handle of the pail. *Think of those times when someone offered to help you carry your burdens and you could not accept their offer. What held you back from receiving?*

The afternoon sun dips behind a cloud, the winds across the ocean whip the waves into a frenzy, but you and the child plod on. A storm looms overhead as the waves begin to pound at your legs. You clutch the treasures tightly, holding them secure from the howling wind. The child struggles to keep his/her footing, when a huge wave engulfs you both. The child disappears under the tow of the water as you emerge from the salty blast. Your heart thumps as you scan the sea for a sign of the little one. Still clutching the pail of treasured mementos, you suddenly let go as you dive into the waters to find the lost one. Your leg brushes against something soft and you grab, catching the child's hair in your hand. You pull the little one up out of the waters and hold her/him close, realizing how grateful your heart is, because this one who seemed lost has been rescued. Across the water you catch a glimpse of your now empty bucket floating away on the rushing waves. You realize where your real treasure lies. *When you have experienced a sobering situation of life and death, how have your priorities been put straight? What are the real treasures in your life?*

༄

The Real Treasures
Write about your feelings and thoughts as you experienced this meditation.

IMAGINATION

I magination is that human capacity to move us beyond our selves. Our deepest longing to make meaning out of existence fuels the imagination to envision what is familiar and what is unfamiliar. Each time we image what can be, each time we envision our dreams, we discover patterns and meaning. This is our incredible capacity to create, to take the visible, ordinary world of every day and see in it a vision for the future. This tremendous capacity of the mind, heart and soul allows us to have access to what is not readily observable. Thus, the power of imagination takes us on the journey of transformation, for we begin to act out of our imagined vision of life, its meaning and its source.

Take, for example, the world of a child's play: dolls, pencils, a chalkboard, fire engines, and trains take a child into a world of adult dreams of being a mommy or a firefighter, a schoolteacher, or an engineer. Adults unconsciously use the capacity to imagine to envision a world at peace, the perfect job, and a sense of family life to play out roles and values in actual time. We are greatly influenced by what we imagine. Images from the media, books, history, and religion all impact the way we view life and the way we live it out.

In the spiritual realm, religious images of God, the Divine, the Creator, greatly influence our behaviors. A judging Deity causes moral action out of a sense of fear. When we outgrow this childlike image of a God to be feared, oftentimes religion will be rejected. But for those whose images of God develop and are honed by deeper, more mature images, religion can become an important force on the journey of the soul. When we fail to image God, we find ourselves estranged from the creative source of our being. We can become cynical, agnostic or even spiritually void.

Images of God are hidden in the depths of our being. Often we don't realize what these images are or if they are helping or hindering our spiritual growth. Growth on the spirit walk invites us to intentionally bring these hidden images of the Source of Our Being into the fore. These images are the language of the soul. Our heart responds to the constant presence of God in each moment, leaving us a legacy of impressions to help us imagine who God is and what God is like.

&&

Imagine God's Presence
Relive an experience that was life-changing for you. Use your imagination to sense how God was present in this situation. After spending time focused on your feelings, your thoughts, and your impressions, ask yourself: *What does my imagination reveal to me about the nature of God—the Source of Being?*

WINTER'S FACE OF GOD

The cold bluster of wind
  curled icy fingers around tightly shut windows
on that night—alone
    in the deep darkness of the cozy house.
Winter's wind relentless
    in her need to enter the closed space of my soul.
It was a long hard journey
    these agonizing two years
      of loss and pain that ached my heart,
    damping the fires of my soul—
        wretched, wreck of a woman
      was I this stormy night. With nothing to console,
    even the flicker of talking heads on the TV
        seemed too much to take,
      so I sat in the dark and listened.

Howling wind matched the cries of my soul
    as I sank deeper into a reverie of remembering.
Loss so great it cracked open the raw wound in my spirit—
    death, children gone, alone—so lonely I saw myself
        wandering in a white landscape of whirling snow,
    tears frozen down my face as I howled to the heavens.
Then came the touch that melted this frozen spirit woman;
    an embrace of One so warm. Soft billowy pillows
      to sink my head on the breast of this One
      who held me close,
        stroking my head and soothing my heart,

until I could open my eyes to the brilliant light of Love
that filled the empty spaces between each cell
and ignite the fires of my spirit once again.

Alone with God

Think about the moments of being achingly alone when you cried out for help. This being some call God is present even in these moments. Imagine yourself in the divine embrace. *Write about your experience in a journal or create a poem to describe the images that come to mind in your reflection.*

SO THIS IS HEAVEN

Children have a way of imagining that strips away all the nuances and contrivances of our culture. Their sense of the unfamiliar is clean and innocent, teaching us more about the realities of the Spirit than our adult minds can perceive. When asked to draw pictures of God they tend to create remarkable and revealing images of the Divine. When asked about heaven they describe a place where there is enough ice cream and candy to send one into a sugar attack.

On one occasion, my niece Allison, who was about five years old, was dealing with the death of her great grand-mother. Her parents explained that she had died and went to heaven. When she arrived at the wake with her family in tow, Allison was quite taken aback. She walked through a doorway into a room filled with flowers. The aroma of the blossoms in these lovely arrangements penetrated every molecule of air. Overwhelmed, the child stepped back, looked up at her mom and dad, and said, "So this is heaven!"

Two young children, ages seven and ten, knelt at the front of the coffin which held their beloved papa. They looked, taking in every detail of his appearance. One placed a fishing lure in his waxy hand and the other tucked a disposable camera into his pocket. They then each kissed his cheek and walked to the back of the parlor, turning to wave good-bye as they reached the door. When asked what they put into the coffin, they replied, "Grandpa's best fishing lure, because he will need it in heaven, and a camera to take a picture of the big fish he will be catching. Heaven is the place where you can do what you like best."

After All

Using your imagination, think about your vision of the afterlife. *What does this say about your image of God? How does this picture of heaven keep you going each day?*

THE WINTER SEASON OF THE SOUL

This winter marks the passing
  of midlife
    as I begin this stretch
      of soul trekking named winter.
That time called old age,
    elderly, second childhood,
      senior moments, the ripe age
    of a venerable soul is my moniker.

A time that compresses the
    generation gap in that going
      back to the wonder of childhood.
May my heart be open to receive
    the wisdom and innocence of the little ones.

A time of no voice when none is needed
    for the rich silences on the backyard swing
      or porch perch in the front
    watching the storm clouds and gulping in
      the cold, frigid air—a bit
crazy to be out like this in the dead of winter.
But I know that winter is not dead—
    the living stuff of green growing things
      rests just under the earth, feeding
        and sleeping in solid, stiff, frozen ground.
The ground into which I soon
    shall rest, buried in bowels that harbor
      life anew. Where am I
headed these winter times of my soul, when
    all seems silent, soft and serene?

Back to the Source of my very being, into whose
    image I have been honed these long years
        of traveling the sacred ground of this earth;
Back to the place I was meant to inhabit,
    winding my way through life's maze of joy and pain—
My own Eden garden, the bounty prepared
    into a banquet of delight, that lies still and deep
        under winter's cover of deep, rich, moanings.

Imagine Afterlife

As you think about the end of your life, recall those
winter times when what appeared dead and dark
was really teeming with life. *What can you imagine
about the afterlife? What experiences have honed you
to face the Source of your being?*

CREATING QUILTS, CREATIVE SOULS

Once we return to that wonderful self we've denied for so long we become interested in going beyond mere selfish pursuits to experience ourselves as part of something greater. This vision of something more—beyond our present day-to-day reality—is an important ingredient to the creative process. Women as a group are fast approaching this creative moment. It all begins with caring for one's needs; physical, intellectual, emotional, and spiritual. As whole persons we have the capacity to create. This human capacity for creativity is part of the cosmic act of co-creating with the Creator to make all things new. I have witnessed this transformation in others as they learned the art of creating a quilt.

This metaphor of quilting helps us grapple with the notion of creativity. There are a multiplicity of pieces that go into the pattern of a quilt. The process of sewing small bits of fabric to create an intricate design opens one to relinquish perfection and enjoy the freedom of knowing and accepting our imperfect self. Flawed, broken and fragmented, we create a pattern nonetheless, a design that is unique and integrated into a whole. Quilting instructs the soul; when we release the need to be perfect we cultivate a new freedom to be spontaneous and creative.

The monotony of sewing strips of fabric together or of running stitches through the layers of a quilt in swirls and shapes affords the serenity of silent spaces in the hurried frenzy of modern living. The sky is the limit; one can sew just about anything into a quilt: flowered shapes, spirals, words, and abstract images. Just as the creating of a quilt opens up a new freedom of imagining and envisioning, the life of the soul has unlimited potential. When we flounder on the interior patterns of the spirit, we find new reservoirs of power to transform the threads of our unique individuality, joining them to the threads of others. Together, we become a woven sampler of patterns and shapes that adorn a barren worldscape with beauty and flourish.

⚜

The Art of Soul

Think about the ways in which you create. Look at the creative process and discover lessons for the art of creating your soul. *What might these parallels be like in your creative experiences?*

IF I COULD PAINT

If I could paint I would sit out on
the swing in the middle of
    winter and choose the softest blue
to color the sky, dotted with swirls of
    clouds to remind me
of the soft hold you have on me—never
    hemming me in or limiting my intuitive,
    impetuous ways.
I would select white for the snow, pure and translucent
    with the hues of azure, magenta, saffron
    imbedded in the pigment, for all the exotic
magical ways you teach my heart to leap
    when you come into my presence.
The rich and ruddy browns, rusty red, and gleaming black
    would etch out the tall bark of trees that
    stand solid and true as you have done for me
all these years together.
Here and there I would lightly sketch
    the fuzzy heads of bush
and rock, logs and odd shapes that
    protrude through the snow—all the
ways you soothed away the fuzziness of my confusion
    with tracings of conversation, understanding,
    sustenance, and reassurance.
The fern green of the conifers, lacing the horizon
    with prickly needles that punctuate my life
    in fresh pine scents, would be my choice

to take me back to times of your strong,
protective embrace, shielding me from
fears that dance around my head
in the middle of the night.
If I could paint this winter scene
it would be you
joined to me that would create my work of art.

֍

An Intimate Work of Art

Think about the influence of your intimate relationships in your journey of growth into the spirit
person you have become. *Name some of the ways
intimacy has created you into a work of art.*

SWEET AND BITTERSWEET

As winter drones on sheer joy can be found in the hope prompted by buckets hung from sugar maples in our village square. The steady plop, plop of sap dropping into steel buckets hanging from a spike in the frozen bark curls my lips in anticipation of sugary syrup. Frigid nights and sun-warmed days herald the end of this season and bring a sweet harvest. But many of the trees are old. Sugar maples planted in the 1800s are in a last-gasp effort to produce more seeds. But the lifeblood sap of the trees' energy is tapped for sugary delights.

As I drive past the gleaming buckets on a sunny day, the snowscape is quiet enough to hear the cries of these ancient ones. They give their all, pierced by steel tubes that drain the coursing sap. Paved roads hem in roots. Removed from their natural forest habitat, the maples suffocate in the pollution of cars and trucks. Salt from winter roads poisons their cells and still they produce the stuff of our breakfast syrup. Tapping continues to bleed these ancient trees of their energy, further weakening them.

The villagers, torn between tradition, profit and concern, begin to notice. Is it too late for these ancient ones? They hear the cries and cut back on the tapping buckets. They plant new saplings in lieu of the death of these old trees. Scientists try saving the trees by injecting the roots of some with mychorrhizal fungi, organisms found in the forest. But the tapping must move on to younger sugar maples while we make sacred the old ones in their last dying years. Signs of hope—sugar sweetness, but what of the cost? Is the tradition of tapping worth the death of these aged maples?

๛

The Price We Pay
Think of the cost, the price paid for neglecting
the aged and taking for granted nature's resources.
What action can you take to honor nature in all the
ways she gives and is sapped by human needs? How
can you become more aware of the self-giving among
the elderly in order to reverence their wisdom?

WINTER'S DANCE

Spirit walk is more a dance
of bending and whirling,
   yielding and releasing,
   letting go and receiving.
The clutched fist of hanging on attachment—owning,
   hoarding and manipulating—swirls in the dizzying
   flurry of white flakes, into oblivion; landing wherever,
   twirled in wind drafts piled high, only to melt away.
Like the dance this season bares
   the spirit to receive whatever goodness or pain
      cued into the complexity of our lives,
      loosening the grip of control.
Days fluctuate from sunlit spaciousness
   to closed tight hibernation as our hearts
      seek to embrace each moment, each situation,
   with peaceful hearts and open hands.
So dance then, in your etched white intricacy,
   yielding, bowing,
   stepping, turning,
   releasing, holding.
Let the rigid, frozen shape of your soul
   melt in an organic, living sequence of movement
      that is liberating and poised to receive.

❦

To Dance Gracefully
As you reflect upon the grace and beauty of the
dance this season, what lessons about letting go can
you enumerate? How do your attachments and need
to control keep you from grace-full dancing?

CELEBRATE THE LIGHT

Try this ritual to celebrate the wisdom that has transformed your spiritual path.

৪৩৪৩ To Prepare

Gather several votive candles to surround your sacred space. You will need matches to light the candles and your journal or a tablet of blank paper and a pen.

৪৩৪৩ The Ritual

Begin by darkening the room. Sit in silence in the dark for a while, listening to the silence and taking in the rich, velvet blackness. Allow your mind to wander over your life, especially the recent past, noting the richness of spirit you have within. Push aside any distracting thoughts, focusing on your inner journey and what you have learned about yourself. As a specific memory, word or phrase comes persistently to the fore, light one candle and write down the spiritual wisdom that has changed your way of looking at life's meaning. Reflect on the losses in your life, the experiences and relationships you have had to surrender to the Highest Power. Light another candle and write about the emptying experience of surrender and the increased capacity of your soul. Continue to use your memory and imagination in this way to brighten your sacred space with candlelight as you name and give thanks for the wisdom you have uncovered in your deepest self through the experiences and encounters of your life. When you have finished, know that you can repeat this ritual at any time. Sit in the light of the candle, taking in the warmth and glow, allowing this gentle radiance to permeate your depths.